War on Sark

War on Sark

The Secret Letters of Julia Tremayne

Introduction by **Michael Beaumont** Seigneur of Sark

Webb & Bower
EXETER, ENGLAND

Published in Great Britain 1981 by
Webb & Bower (Publishers) Limited
33 Southernhay East, Exeter, Devon EX1 1NS

Designed by Vic Giolitto

Picture research by Anne-Marie Ehrlich

Copyright © Xan Franks 1981

British Library Cataloguing in Publication Data

Tremayne, Julia
  War on Sark
  1. World War, 1939–1945 – Personal narratives,
  British
  2. Sark – Social life and customs
  1. Title
  942.3′45′0840924

  ISBN 0-906671-41-8

Phototypeset by Man Photocomposition,
Keyspools (IOM) Ltd., Onchan, Isle of Man

Printed and bound in Great Britain by
Hazell, Watson and Viney Limited, Aylesbury, Buckinghamshire

Contents

Introduction
Michael Beaumont Seigneur of Sark

Sark, the fourth largest of the Channel Islands lies about one hundred miles south of Weymouth, seven miles from Guernsey and just twenty-two miles off the French coast which is clearly visible on a fine day. The Islands are geographically part of France but became a British Crown possession by the fortunes of war. In mediaeval times they belonged to the great Duchy of Normandy and were part of the estates of William the Conqueror and successive Norman Kings. In later years, notably under King John, the British lost all their Norman possessions with the exception of the Channel Islands which remained loyal to the Crown.

The Norman heritage is still apparent to this day in law, custom and place-names and, although English is now almost universally used except for formal occasions, the change from Norman French has been made within the space of one life-span.

Sark is just two square miles in area and has a resident population of approximately 550, not dissimilar to a small English hamlet. It stands three hundred feet above sea level surrounded by forty-two miles of rugged cliffs embracing a quiet, varied scenery of small banked and hedged fields, wooded valleys and cliff-land covered with wild flowers. There is no village as such, and although the shops tend to be congregated in one area, the houses and farmsteads are in little groups spread over the Island, built where water was plentiful or where a natural dip in the land or a valley provides shelter.

Transport is by horse and carriage, bicycle or by foot, and as there are no motor cars the roads are surfaced with crushed stone which gives a good smooth surface but is a little dusty in summer and muddy in winter. Tractors, the only motorized transport allowed, are now commonly used for agriculture and carting but are a recent innovation and were scarce at the beginning of the War.

Although tourism was the principal industry at the outbreak of the War and remains so today, the Island is extensively farmed. There are mainly dairy cattle but also some sheep, pigs and hens with the arable devoted largely to potatoes and food and pasture for the animals. During the War farming was of necessity more intensive, growing wheat, barley and enough potatoes to export to Guernsey. Fishing forms the third major industry and catches of mackerel, whiting, lobsters and crabs are generally plentiful.

There was no electricity in Sark at the time of the War except for private generator sets in one or two of the large houses and hotels. There were, and are, no street lights, and home lighting was by oil-lamp and candle. There were no means of pumping water except by hand-pump and water was carried in buckets from the wells. There was no running water, flush lavatories were almost non-existent and bathing was in a tub in front of the fire. A generating station was set up in Sark by private enterprise in 1947 and it is now difficult to realize the difference electricity has made to everyday life.

Sark is entirely self-supporting and self-governing under a mediaeval feudal system introduced in 1565. Many years before the inhabitants had been driven out by various raiders, and the Island had become deserted except as a refuge for pirates and French privateers. The potential danger of this was causing trouble to local shipping, and considerable disquiet to the neighbouring Islands, so the premier Seigneur of Jersey, Helier de Carteret, proposed that he be granted the Island of Sark as an adjunct to his own fief (feudal land holding) in Jersey to establish a new permanent settlement. This request was granted and confirmed by Letters Patent from Queen Elizabeth I.

By the terms of these Letters Patent the Seigneur was required to maintain at least forty men for the defence of the Island and pay to the Crown a rent of one-twentieth part of a knight's fee per annum. In return he was given all the rights, privileges and obligations of a mediaeval Seigneur which included among many others the rights to lease land, tithes, the sole right to grind corn, the streams, all minerals, flotsam and jetsam, and to set up a court. This form of landholding had long since been superseded in England but was still applicable in the Channel Islands at that time.

To ensure that he could always muster forty armed men de Carteret divided Sark into forty landholdings and for a small annual *rente* of chickens, wheat and barley gave the land in perpetuity to forty families. To give the new settlers a say in Island affairs he formed his parliament, known as Chief Pleas, from the heads of the forty families.

Sark is still ruled by the terms of this Elizabethan Charter. The

Seigneur still pays an annual *rente* to the Crown of 'one-twentieth part of a knight's fee'; he should still be able to raise forty men armed with muskets; he receives *rente* reckoned in chicken, wheat and barley; and Chief Pleas is made up of the owners of the forty land-holdings, though they have now been augmented by twelve elected deputies to represent those inhabitants other than the landowners.

The Island is governed through Chief Pleas and makes its own laws and raises its own taxes, though these must in certain cases have the sanction of the Queen in Council. Law is maintained by two unpaid constables elected each year by Chief Pleas and justice is administered by a Court composed of the Seneschal (Magistrate), Prévôt (Sheriff) and Greffier (Clerk to the Court), all of whom are appointed by the Seigneur.

The Island came into my family in 1852 with Royal consent when the previous Seigneurial family went bankrupt in a silver-mining venture that left a forebear of mine as principal creditor. My grandmother, Mrs Sibyl Beaumont (later Mrs Sibyl Hathaway when she remarried after the death of my grandfather), inherited the Island in 1927 and was Dame of Sark (the female title) for forty-seven years until her death at the age of ninety in 1974.

Sibyl Hathaway was a remarkable woman by any standards. Highly intelligent, a forceful personality, with a strong sense of humour and quite fearless, she was the dominant figure in any gathering. Her character and unique status ensured that the world's Press gave her and the Island considerable publicity over the years. Many of the laws, past and present, were attributed quite erroneously to her personally and it was not uncommon to see head-lines such as 'The Dame bans divorce', or 'The Dame bans motor cars', and so on.

Her personality gave her the qualities necessary to lead Sark through the trials of occupation with the minimum of hardship, qualities officially recognized by the award from Her Majesty the Queen of the OBE and later the DBE.

In 1940 the population of the Island was about 470 and was made up principally of Sarkees but with a sizeable proportion of retired or semi-retired British subjects. The Islands, being within shelling range of the French coast, were quite indefensible and, very wisely, the British Government declared the Islands 'open' and offered to evacuate all who wished to leave.

My grandmother called a meeting of the inhabitants and explained as best she could the advantages and disadvantages of departing for England. She warned of all the hardships ahead but stated that she and Mr Hathaway had no intention of leaving, and advised all those with property or landholdings to stay and weather the storm. The result was that a few of the English decided to leave but all the Sark people remained.

The Germans arrived on Sark on July 3rd, 1940, confident of moving on to England in the near future. The first few months were uneventful, but then the military administration was passed over to the Civil Affairs Officer and the restrictions began in earnest, and were gradually increased over the years as the tide of war moved against them.

Agriculture and fishing (under supervision) were encouraged with a proportion of all the produce earmarked for the German garrison. A curfew was imposed and the cliffs and beaches extensively mined. Essential commodities such as seed for agricultural crops and fuel for the fishing boats were imported from France but certain foods, clothing and cooking fuel other than wood became unobtainable. Fuel for the lamps soon ran out and with the restriction of the curfew people lived by daylight hours.

Eventually the workmen had no boots, and the children had the toes cut out of their shoes to make them long enough and some went barefoot. There was no soap for two years and the only hot water was that heated over a wood fire so it was a wonder that no epidemic broke out, although the children did suffer from scabies, lice and impetigo.

In many ways Sark was the most fortunate of the Channel Islands as it had no town population to support. It never experienced the building of vast concrete fortifications and the importation of hundreds of Organization Todt workers and, later, Russian prisoners of war necessary for this work. Nevertheless there was a garrison of two hundred officers and men to be maintained on the Island.

The Commando raids on Dieppe and Sark made the Germans nervous and brought on new restrictions and the planting of more minefields. It is also thought that these caused the deportations of most of the English residents including women and children, and men up to seventy years of age. No official explanation was ever given but it was commonly believed to be purely a form of revenge.

Conditions deteriorated considerably after the Allied landings in France as the Islands became completely isolated. The Germans, then numbering about two hundred, demanded more and more of the produce so hunger became a very real issue and actual starvation a possibility. At last in January 1945 a Red Cross ship brought in food parcels and these arrived in sufficient numbers for each man, woman and child to have one parcel a fortnight, and the joy and gratitude the people felt for their parcels were indescribable.

After the arrival of the Red Cross parcels the Germans demanded even more of the local produce, but they became more hungry than the Islanders to an extent that some would come round to doors after curfew begging for food. They started to steal vegetables, pigs and chickens and even cats and dogs, although they were severely punished if caught. It is to the Germans' credit that they never interfered with the distribution of the food parcels.

Viewed in retrospect and with knowledge of how other communities suffered under occupation, the local people were not badly treated although no excuse can be made for the deportations. When the Germans first arrived they were confident of victory and wanted to create a good impression; then, as the tide turned and defeat became a possibility, they feared they might be punished if they had treated the people badly. Their discipline was good throughout and though it declined in the last few months it remained remarkably high considering they were worse off physically and morally than the Islanders. Had discipline broken, the ending might have been very different.

I was at school in England during the War so was fortunately spared the deprivations and traumas suffered by the inhabitants of Sark. I heard subsequently of the hardships and hunger and could see for myself the effect on my grandmother whose weight had dropped from ten to seven stone. I heard many stories and anecdotes and still do from time to time as the memories are still fresh in the minds of Sark people. But these stories are naturally told with hindsight so I find the letters of Mrs Tremayne extremely interesting as they include all the rumours and all the fears of what might have been, which are not remembered in later years or at any rate not related. I hope and pray Sark never has to face such times again.

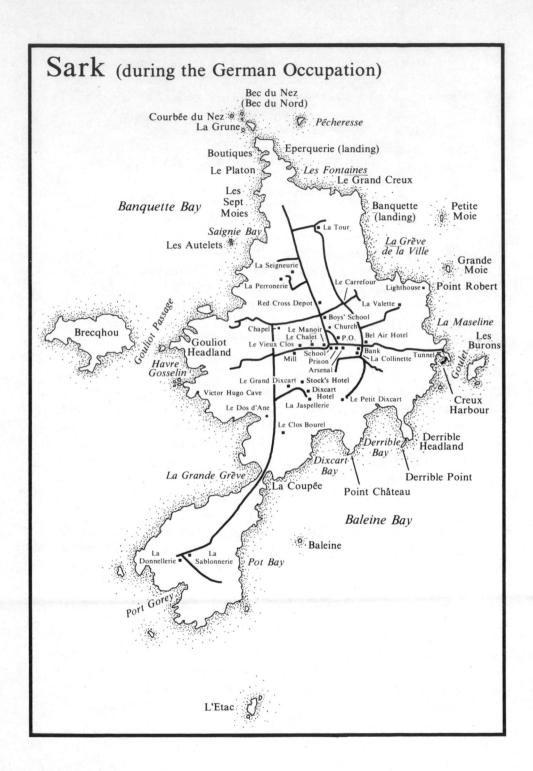

Sark (during the German Occupation)

Bec du Nez
(Bec du Nord)

Courbée du Nez
La Grune

Pécheresse

Eperquerie (landing)

Boutiques

Les Fontaines

Le Platon

Le Grand Creux

Les
Sept
Moies

Banquette
(landing)

Petite
Moie

Banquette Bay

La Tour

Saignie Bay

*La Grève
de la Ville*

Les Autelets

La Seigneurie

Grande
Moie

La Perronerie

Le Carrefour

Red Cross Depot

Lighthouse

Point Robert

La Valette

Boys' School

La Maseline

Brecqhou

Chapel

Church

Le Manoir
Le Chalet

P.O.

Bel Air Hotel

Les
Burons

Gouliot Passage

Gouliot
Headland

Le Vieux Clos

Mill

School
Prison
Arsenal

Bank
La Collinette

Tunnel

Goulet

*Havre
Gosselin*

Le Grand Dixcart

Stock's Hotel

Dixcart
Hotel

Le Petit Dixcart

Creux
Harbour

Victor Hugo Cave

Le Dos d'Ane

La Jaspellerie

Le Clos Bourel

*Derrible
Bay*

Derrible
Headland

*Dixcart
Bay*

Derrible Point

La Grande Grève

La Coupée

Point Château

Baleine Bay

Baleine

La
Donnellerie

La
Sablonnerie

Pot Bay

Port Gorey

L'Etac

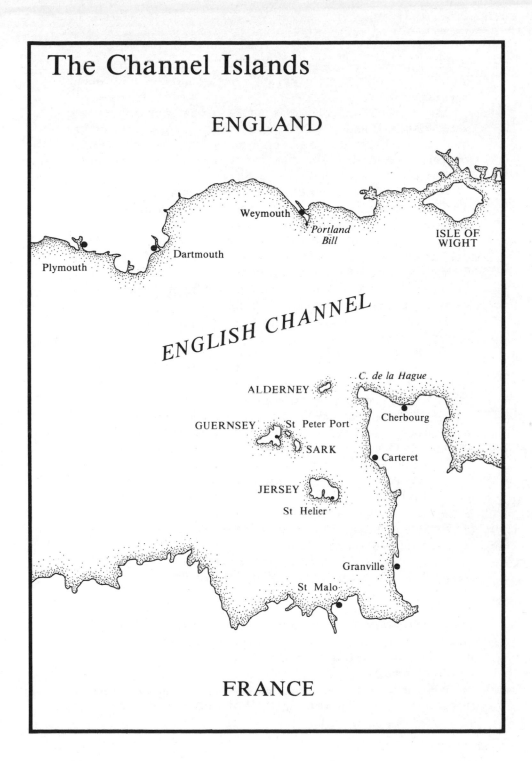

The Channel Islands

ENGLAND

Weymouth

*Portland
Bill*

ISLE OF
WIGHT

Plymouth

Dartmouth

ENGLISH CHANNEL

C. de la Hague

ALDERNEY

GUERNSEY   St Peter Port

Cherbourg

SARK

Carteret

JERSEY

St Helier

Granville

St Malo

FRANCE

July 1st, 1940

We have been invaded by the enemy in Jersey and Guernsey and all communications cut off.

The towns of Jersey, Guernsey and Alderney were demilitarized on the 20th, 21st and 22nd of June; every troop was taken from the three Islands. I suppose the Government thought it best to do so. It was only on Saturday 29th June that it was made known on the wireless that they were open towns.

In the meantime, on Friday 28th June at about 7pm, we heard the Germans coming in earnest. Never will I forget the flight over this house on their way to bomb Guernsey harbour, and the terrible machine-gunning all the way. Norah was out shopping and she, together with lots who were caught in the lanes so suddenly, got into ditches and hedges for cover. Mary Watts had the bullets on her roof but no damage was done in Sark except fright, no panic—dear old Mrs Falle at the pavilion died of fright.

The death toll in Guernsey was very heavy and lots of the injured have since died.

You know what a busy little town St Peter Port is, especially on the White Rock when all the carts and lorries are drawn up to get their produce on the cargo boats. The mail-boat was already in and passengers and refugees buying their tickets at the office when those devilish huns showed in sight and began to bomb unmercifully. The White Rock and all around were a perfect shambles. It only lasted one hour in Guernsey but the panic and loss of life was great, then they came madly rushing back over our lovely Isle, scattering things all the way. We made a cubby-hole in the hall, under the stairs, until all was quiet.

Norah eventually arrived home, white and breathless. You must not forget that although the larger Islands have gas masks, shelters, etc., we have no protection at all.

Here, Norah and I are trying to keep cool and collected: there is plenty of food on the Island, lots of cattle to kill if necessary, rabbits, chickens, eggs, milk, plenty of butter and cream. Our ration books are no use at present because we are even cut off from Guernsey. No boats are allowed to go or come, except perhaps a lifeboat from Guernsey to bring a doctor or midwife across. There was quite a panic here and the Island doctor left us without a bit of warning. Our biggest hardship is being cut off from the mainland.

We had been packed up some days and meant to cross over, then came that terrible raid on the White Rock, and next day the invasion.

ays, I can tell you, we
In Jersey we hear that
s much more rigid. I
anding and some folks

over the Bel Air, and
Miss, when I walk past

r I firmly believe when
hings over as there are
£5 in hens some time
rts. We are, as you will
take the surplus and
God they cannot ship
cows can be fed.
Germans' consent must
are raiding our shops
l sorts. That is so much
ew mark notes, which

has been sent from
folk, and Colinette is
ach, and beautiful fruit.
o send any more away.
!

le to send *one* wire to
ow pleased I shall be to
e expected under the

, real heavy ones, also a
have been deafening.
are, I do hope you are
times. I wish I had a
Please God our troubles
on. If I didn't have my
. We are doing a bit of
not know if that will be
tart turning my clothes

July 2nd, 1940

All day since 5am planes have been flying over us, some almost touching the tree tops, carrying troops to Guernsey. Some say there are 2,000 there, no troops have come to Sark yet, we can only wonder what is going to happen and hope for the best. Work is going on as usual in the gardens and the harbour works are carrying on if they can get the cement, none of the Sark men have gone or been conscripted, I suppose because the Islands are open towns.

Miss MacEwan has been in and is in great distress because she cannot get away to her beloved Scotland, but in the midst of our loneliness we can see the funny side and have a good laugh occasionally. She sent us into fits of laughter when she told us, as soon as she heard of the invasion, how she proceeded to pack her bag and hoped that when the Germans arrived here they would take her back in the returning boat. The said bag already packed and tied up, she proceeded to the Bel Air Hotel to find Dulcie, and the two thought they would be greatly strengthened by a nip of Scotch. I think the nip must have been very prolonged, because getting very tired of waiting for the said boat (which has not arrived yet) she returned to her cottage. She then suddenly remembered she had hidden her money in the garden and started frantically digging for it. By then the Scotch had taken such a hold that half the garden was ploughed up before it was found, she had quite forgotten the hiding place.

If you had heard her tell the tale you would have laughed until you cried, I did, and it did me the world of good.

July 3rd, 1940

A lifeboat arrived in Sark this morning bringing about ten German soldiers and a Corporal, they had lunch at the Seigneurie and are to be billeted at the Bel Air (which is empty). Everybody says they seem very nice and if we keep to all the rules laid down, things will go on much as usual. No one must be out after 11pm, no spirits sold in hotels, only beer, all guns to be given up, the national anthem is not to be sung. We can go to church or chapel. German money is to be used, and worst of all the swastika is flying over the Bel Air. Who would have thought we would have lived to see that in this beautiful little Island that I have loved for nearly forty years and you have all known since you were babies.

July 4th, 1940

Everything today seems quieter and we are g
less worried, there are no planes overhead and
We can go to bed and sleep in peace every nigl
are all thankful for is that we can keep our wire
it would have been misery not to know what En

Today we hear we can go to Guernsey if n
permitted to write. A boat brought some mea
had been without about ten days. Mrs Hatha
bought all the stores up from the Elizabeth and
and elsewhere. It was pathetic in Guernsey how
houses and flew to the boat, distracted. They w
without food, waiting their turn on the jetty. N
went and almost every nurse, and patients wei
Shops were left open, no assistants, and a gene
prevailed. The homes, farms and cows etc. ar
State. It is not so in Sark, all goes according to
being cut off we are quite happy.

July 5th, 1940

I expect the German troops are revelling in the
good Sark butter, home-killed meat, home-mad
milk and the shops well-stocked. Miss Durant (
roaring trade in the village receiving nice new c
notes; Lanyon, the baker, is just as busy.

It is not good to hear on the wireless of all tl
parts of England, I feel I have no business to go
night and sleep a peaceful sleep when so many a
in peril.

Miss Carter is still with us. She has no wish
cottage, it is right on the coast (near the lighthouse

July 6th, 1940

It is only a week since we were cut off. I do not
known such a wonderful year for roses and our g
especially with the ramblers on the arches. We h
first for months and it is very refreshing. I hav
beans, potatoes and salads, lots of loganberries
crop coming on, and every cottage and house
towards helping the food supply.

behaving ourselves, mum's the word nowad
are all afraid of the rules being tightened up.
the curfew is at 7.30: awful! and the rule
suppose they tried to keep the Germans from
say there was hand-to-hand fighting.

It is very hurtful to see the swastika flyin
poor Tonette, who was in the last war, says,
I turn my head away so as not to see it'.

We have been raiding the shops today, f
the stocks are sold out we shall get very few
no English boats. I am so thankful I investe
ago and my garden is well planted with all so
know, controlled by the Germans, they ma
send it to Germany, especially butter. Than
the milk so we can always have that, while th

If a pig, cow or calf has to be killed, the
be obtained, and they must be present. The
for cocoa and chocolate, clothes, soap and a
the less for us, and they are giving crisp r
might easily prove worthless after the war.

Great excitement, a ton of tomatoe
Guernsey to be distributed amongst us Sa
quite busy doling them out, quite a nice lot e
They have tons in Guernsey and are unable
What a loss to one of their greatest industrie

July 10th, 1940

Another bit of excitement—we *may* be ab
friends in England, it is not certain yet, but I
let you know we are happy as can b
circumstances.

Today has been a day of thunder storm
battle seems to be going on at sea, the report

We wonder how you are, and where yo
keeping well these hard and nerve-rackin
carrier pigeon to send you a note each day.
will grow less and we shall see a light so
chickens and my garden I would go barm
Red Cross work at the Hall, but one does
forbidden as time goes on, then I must
inside out and upside down.

Sometimes I think the war will end quickly, and *soon*, so the only thing is to be careful and try to make others so. There is going to be great distress in the Islands because so many people (English residents) have pensions and their money is in England and it will not come through, Auntie Annie and Miss Carter, for example. Miss Carter is still with us, and pays while she can. She will have to owe me what she cannot pay, until after the war, it is all so perplexing but we are all determined to help each other and stick together like a big family. There will be no money soon to pass round. That will be the time to try us, to test our endurance.

As the time goes on I keep wondering how you are, and do so hope you are not worrying about us.

July 11th, 1940

Nothing very exciting has happened today. Planes go frantically over the house but we can hear so little news of dear old England.

We hear today that we can have communication with Jersey and all people who were in the other Islands when invaded will be allowed to go home. Alderney is a desert Island, everyone was taken off and every bit of livestock and provisions of all kinds were brought to Guernsey.

July 12th, 1940

A dull, cold day. The log fire is very welcome and knitting and sewing are well to the fore. We have written to Guernsey for some wool in case we are cut off for the winter, Heaven forbid, I pray for an early peace.

There is no petrol in Guernsey, buses are stopped and all cars and bicycles are at a premium. The growers and porters are coming over to Sark frequently and buying up all the horses. The people who want to get to the country parishes in Guernsey have to go in horse-vans, or walk, so we are back to Victorian days. There was a wedding in Guernsey this week and the bride went to church in one of those quaint chairs, like a hansom cab.

July 13th, 1940

The planes are very busy overhead, some extremely low, they terrify me, and I am always at the very bottom of the vegetable garden, or feeding the chicks, when they go so low. How I do pity the people who have them overhead continually, day and night. I do think of you a lot and poor Auntie Betty, our nerves won't stand it as we get older. I am OK and try to keep very busy. We had another ton of tomatoes sent over from Guernsey and they were divided equally among our 450 residents. I am bottling a great many for the winter.

The shopkeepers are forbidden to sell candles, not even one, and salt is rationed, we get 2oz each. Butter is not as plentiful as it once was.

July 14th, 1940

We hear that 500lb of Sark and Guernsey butter was being taken to Germany and the plane crashed near Herm, several planes have come down around the Islands.

Today, Sunday, is wonderfully calm, not much sign of any activity, we are longing to hear Mr Churchill's speech tonight at 9pm. I hope he sends a message to the Channel Islands, it will be cheering for us. This seems unbelievable, the Germans have been in occupation nearly three weeks, and I have not seen one yet. Not getting any mail is one of our biggest hardships. I did say when stamps went up to $2\frac{1}{2}$d that I should not write so much to anyone, well, I have more than eaten my words!

I went down to see Pattie and Willie of the valley last evening and they are both as gay as larks, the war does not trouble them and they are so confident of victory that it was quite a tonic.

July 15th, 1940

We heard Mr Churchill's speech last evening, no mention of wee Sark or the Islands. I cannot think how they can forget us entirely, for we are all British. It gave me a pain when he said that the war might go on until 1942, the food shortage would be acute by then, unless the Red Cross bring us some. We might become like Hitler and begin eating the carpets, God forbid. The Sarkees are so calm and collected about it all, nothing worries them so far.

It is with bitterness we read in the Guernsey papers (only the size of a pocket handkerchief now) different notices which end, 'by the kind permission of the German Commander.'

All the men of both Islands have had to hand their guns in, so rabbits will have to be ferreted, fishing is only allowed one mile out to sea and the fishermen say they cannot catch much there.

I have a lot of dead trees that must come down for winter fuel.

We are very lucky to have them, for coal will be like gold. I have not handled any German money yet and don't want any. I hear we are to have another ton of tomatoes sent over to Sark tomorrow, so the Collinette will be alive with people and their baskets. As well as bottling them, I am making tomato sauce and purée and we are having salads galore. We shall all have complexions like a wild rose after a few months of being vegetarians. I hope it will only be months and not years.

The Germans have controlled almost everything, butter, eggs, potatoes, salt, tea, meat and bread. I expect the goods will go over to Germany in great quantities. I really don't know why they invaded these Islands, for, apart from the tomatoes, potatoes and flour industries, there is nothing of any value. Most of the Guernsey potato crop has Colorado beetle. Perhaps Hitler thought there were still silver and copper mines here in Sark. What a hope!

July 16th, 1940

Great activity, planes over in great crowds on their way to England. Mrs Hathaway says she has two tons of wheat crop, and all the farmers have grown quite a lot, also at the Seigneurie there is a mill to grind it. She also brought a ton of flour to be sold or doled out later. When that gives out I hope the war will be over, or peace in sight.

The ladies who have Dixcart Hotel have bought a goat so they get free milk. I must see if I can get one, there is plenty of grass in the meadows, and I must learn to milk it.

I have been making jam today, a mixture of rhubarb, apple and logans. It has turned out quite nicely and is a little more in our cupboard. The vegetable garden yields well and the potato crop looks fine.

July 17th, 1940

Nothing exciting has happened today except they are cutting the corn in the meadows and the tractor is busy. The weather has broken and it is not too warm, we are glad of a fire each evening. I am still knitting for the Red Cross depot. I can never get used to the idea of being under German rule. There is a shortage of wool, no stockings to be had either and soon I suppose, no boots. What a life! Things we had put in the rag-bag we are turning out and making use of again.

July 18th, 1940

We have at last got a doctor for the duration of the war. He is from Jersey, rather elderly and seems very nice, just he and his wife. They are at the Vieux Clos.

July 20th, 1940

I did not write yesterday as it was all quiet and uninteresting, just the daily routine. Today there has been great activity in the air, eighty or a hundred planes flew over, the noise was deafening and simply terrifying. There has been a fight between a German plane and one of our Spitfires at Bec-du-Nord, the German one came down in the sea. We are still allowed to keep our wirelesses, thank goodness. No word yet about the wires and postcards we were told we should be able to send to our relatives.

The north-east coast seems to have nightly visits by the raiders and I know poor Auntie Betty will be worried and nervy.

July 21st, 1940

A glorious Sunday and so quiet and peaceful. How can a war be waging only a few miles from our coast! Norah went to church in the morning and I went in the evening. The chapel folk all come to church now because there is no Wesleyan parson allowed to come over for Sunday duty.

Poor little deserted Alderney has no one on it but German troops. When the inhabitants all left in such a violent hurry, lots of cattle, cats and dogs were shot and left to smell and rot. Now the States of Guernsey are trying to get forty men together who will go and clear it all up and put the houses and hotels in order, also gather in the harvest and bring it back to Guernsey for our use. So far we are short of nothing and with great care I am sure we shall survive the winter.

July 22nd, 1940

I think I told you the lighthouse was closed and all the lighthouse men had gone. Do you remember the huge stone tank of paraffin at the top of the steps, with a pipe and handrail combined, carrying it down hundreds of steps to the lighthouse? Well there are thousands of gallons of oil to be distributed on the Island, so we are all right for light and stoves, and the coal supply is good also. I have ordered some coal today. Miss Carter left us today. She has stayed one month and now she is going to try to get a job in Guernsey for the duration.

July 24th, 1940

We are told that octopus makes a good square meal, but as it is very tough it must be cut into very small pieces and then stewed or fried! I sincerely hope we are not reduced to that. In a farmyard I passed yesterday there were hundreds of pounds of tomatoes dumped down to feed the pigs, what a sin, but it is impossible to get them to England.

They are starting to teach the German language in Guernsey and showing German films, so they must hope to win.

July 25th, 1940

I did not hear Sir Henry Gauvain on the wireless last night talking about Alderney. I believe people were marvellous there, and so calm. One has to be very brave to turn the key in the lock of a home one has had for life and flee at a moment's notice. I still think I have done the best thing by staying here, we are not worried or disturbed in any way by the German troops, they are most polite and get on very well with the Sark people, who they say are so kind and quiet. I believe the people in Jersey set on the Germans with picks and shovels, so their restrictions are much harder than ours in Sark or Guernsey. Some folk say 'Old Haw-Haw' said one night 'Goodnight Guernsey and Sark, goodnight Jersey pigs!'

July 29th, 1940

Nothing of much importance has happened since last week, except I have been having disturbing dreams. I expect it is the fault of going to bed in a worried state. Today I went over to see dear Mr and Mrs Toplis, they are both nearly stone-deaf and are living in a world of their own twenty or thirty years back, they do not know there is a war on, or hear any bombs or raids, they don't even know that Germans are on the Island. What bliss! Their wireless won't go and they get no papers from anywhere.

The bombing here last night was deafening, but we hear no details. I thought we might be taking Cherbourg back but Norah said it was nearer than that, so we wonder if they were bombing

Guernsey or Jersey airport. It is said the German officers and big pots have a plane all ready to fly off if they find things are going against them. The only voice we hear and know is Alvar Liddell on the BBC which is familiar and welcome and I keep on hoping he will give us some message. You will remember he and his wife spent a very happy holiday here last summer and loved Little Sark. 'Believe it or not', (à la Ripley), I have not seen a German yet and our Island is only three miles long, I am rather pleased about it although I hear they are well behaved, we are told to, 'mind our own business and the Germans will mind theirs'. It seems so strange to be in Sark this beautiful summer month of July with August in sight, and not to see a single visitor or any sign of holiday makers, ah, me!

July 31st, 1940

We hear there is to be a bank holiday in Guernsey on Monday. In other years Sark has had a record boating day, often six or seven hundred people for the day—think of those shillings in poll-tax. Goodness knows how the new harbour will be paid for but it is still going on while they can get the cement. The shops are gradually getting less in stock and when Guernsey is sold out we wonder how we shall get along. I try not to worry, but sometimes it is impossible.

I do think they might let us send one telegram to England and get a reply. We are still waiting patiently and are told it must be done through the Red Cross, a lot of red tape.

August 1st, 1940

Here we start another month. Since 1st July a lot seems to have happened in Sark, but now that we have all settled down and got used to the rules and conditions things go on quite smoothly. The winter will be the greatest test, but if we can only keep warm and get enough to eat we shall be thankful.

I have been making tomato cocktail and chutney and all sorts this week, trying to fill the cupboard up with things for the winter, but in my heart I think that Hitler will have climbed down before then, he seems to have come to a brick wall already.

August 2nd, 1940

Hundreds of planes keep flying over us, we know that Cherbourg has been heavily bombed, some say it is in flames, the gun-fire has been terrific night and day. We hear today that a destroyer has been off Guernsey and cut the cable to France, so the German invaders do not appear too safe if the British should surround the coast. We also hear Mr Chervil of Guernsey is to broadcast to England. A copy of his speech is in the evening paper.

August 3rd, 1940

A glorious summer day, blue sky, blue sea and the birds singing everywhere. I did my morning round of shopping, foraging is a better name for it, seeing what the shops *would* sell. All goods are controlled by the Germans. No tin of anything must be sold, although the shops have plenty, especially tinned milk. There is no margarine, no cheese, no bacon and very little flour. I can get very little chicken food and it will grieve me to kill the chickens off, for they have been and still are a source of income. I shall try hard to feed them, but you see we are getting nothing from England or France, and as the shops sell out they cannot be restocked. We get the steamer two or three times a week from Guernsey, but it is mostly cargo for the harbour. I suppose the White Rock in Guernsey looks a very forlorn place. The only porter there is 'Our Gould' who has a white horse and cart, but there are no motors, no buses or petrol, so all the country folk have to walk into town if they have no bikes or a horse and trap.

I hope when the Germans see we are getting short of food, they will clear out. We hear today a French boat has taken all the guns away, so that looks hopeful, also there is talk of the English coming to bomb the airport in Guernsey and Jersey so that no one can land, and so those already here will be in a trap, for our warships are not very far away. Oh, let it be soon!

We are all bright and cheerful, giving and lending each other what the other has not. The carpenter sent us a basket of lovely peaches the other day and Mrs Falle brought us a nice lobster today.

August 4th, 1940

It is just twenty-six years ago that the last war started. I thought perhaps Hitler was staging something for this anniversary, but all has been calm. One wonders what he will do next. Here our boats have been stopped again between Guernsey and Sark so we cannot even get newspapers, and there is a sort of conspiracy in the air; no planes, no guns, or any sounds whatever, and leaflets have been dropped over L'Ancresse telling the Germans to clear out before the airport is bombed. The fishermen have been warned not to go out fishing, so there is a dead stillness everywhere. People who live very close to the airport have been warned to move away. I hope and pray we don't have a bomb on Sark.

August 6th, 1940

I wonder if you are rationed for clothes and boots in England. We are to have new leaflets in our ration books for them and also for boots to be mended. This week they have also rationed soap, meths, paraffin, salt and all sorts. 1oz salt each, 3oz soap a month, either toilet or household. However shall we keep clean?

We hear the German Commandant is getting a peace ball up, to be held at the Royal Hotel on the 19th August, when they apparently will have conquered England. Sark residents are to have a special boat sent for them, free. How nice, and what a hope. They are tightening up all the laws made a month ago, and for disobeying some it is the death penalty. Soon we shall have to ask permission to breathe. We hear on the wireless tonight that letters can be posted from England to the Channel Islands, but they must be unsealed.

Auntie Annie has got her pension allowed by the Guernsey States until we can get into communication with the mainland again. Mrs Babbe offered to keep her for nothing until she could pay, it was awfully kind of her. The Guernsey States are helping everyone in distress. I think it is very good of them, don't you? We are jogging along, so far, so good, not penniless yet, but when the shops are empty our money will be no good. What a heavenly state of affairs! I think I told you we are let off our rent until things improve.

August 8th, 1940

It is perfect bedlam here today and we hear on the wireless there is a big battle in the Channel and on Cherbourg. Planes have been going over in hundreds and the old house fairly rocks with the din. Things are very much worse in Guernsey as water, gas and electricity are scarce. The people are even rationed with water and are told to have baths in a quart of hot water and use no more, so what with the soap shortage we shall all become a dark and dusky race if it goes on long. I believe they are sending all our surplus food to Germany by plane. They have stopped the fishermen going out to fish this week. I wonder if they mean to starve us out.

August 9th, 1940

We believe they are bombing Guernsey and Jersey Airports today, but we cannot get to know anything for certain yet.

If I have to go round with the hat, we must come to England when peace is declared after all this tension.

I am still hanging on to my hens and chickens, for how much longer I don't know, for corn is not to be had.

The communications being cut off with England is a very serious thing. That was not so in the last war. Fortunately we have plenty of vegetables and potatoes so we will have to make potato cakes. I wonder if you will ever read all this tripe I am writing to you, but it is interesting to relate the doings each day.

There are 800 German troops in Guernsey and the States have to provide all the food.

August 10th, 1940

A terrible day. Our planes were bombing Guernsey Airport, more or less all the day until about 9pm. You will probably have heard it on the wireless. I am glad they have made a start, for it might mean we shall be free again very soon. It is only six weeks since they invaded but it seems like six weary months or years. It is so strange to see Sark so empty in such lovely weather instead of the mighty rush and bustle of the holiday crowd.

August 11th, 1940

A glorious summer day, not a cloud in the sky but hundreds of planes going over to England on their devilish errands and the noise is deafening. The Sark people have always been noted for their lackadaisical ways, but it is more so now. Someone said last year Sark was 400 years behind the times, so will this come to their aid now having to do without so many things?

August 12th, 1940

Fishing is still not allowed and the sea is full of fish at this time of the year. The reason is that two men put out in a boat from Guernsey, hoping to get to England and were caught, so all are being punished alike. Also the men cannot go rabbiting because all guns had to be handed in. The Germans do the rabbiting and the eating of them too. The two German chiefs have been called back to Germany although the troops are still here, and we wonder what it means. Perhaps Hitler thinks he is losing or he may want them in a more important place. What a lot of his planes our men are bringing down.

August 13th, 1940

Seventy-eight German planes brought down today, not bad for the 13th! One crashed off Sark late last evening, but as Sark seems off the map and forgotten they won't count that. I hope they finish them off this time and stop some of the Germans' little games. It must be dreadful in England, everywhere, especially these last four days of continual raids. Cherbourg is still being heavily bombed and the coast around France. I should love to get news from Madame S. and how they are faring. Mayenne is in Northern France and she is sure to be with her mother.

August 14th, 1940

Things seem a bit quieter here today, not so many planes overhead. How thankful we are to have the wireless but even that may be taken away if the Germans tighten up the laws as they warn us they will do later. Today they are having a great parade and concert in Candie Grounds and the new German Commander is taking the salute. There is also a rumour that Guernsey Airport is to be bombed again tonight. Let us hope it will happen while the salute is on and that they may be within reach of some shell.

August 15th, 1940

A grand day for Britain—one hundred and sixty planes brought down. Fancy a thousand German planes attacking. The sky here has been black with them. Miss Carter and May Watts had just gone into the water for a swim at Cable Bay, when they began to ascend overhead. I should have loved to have seen Miss Carter's face. I believe she was terrified but Mary never turned a hair and continued swimming quite placidly. Today the weather is thundery. Somehow one does not do one's work at all cheerfully, and the clocks being German time, one hour in advance of summer time, makes everything confused and upset. Curfew is at 11pm and blackout at 10pm and the Germans knock at your door if they see a gleam of light. The penalty is very heavy.

August 16th, 1940

I must begin to go slow with my Diary because I don't know where the next paper will come from. Old Moore says the war will be over in October. Things are not happening as Mr Hitler planned and he did not drink his tea at Buckingham Palace. How I wish I could get at his tea-cup before he put it to his mouth. He would not plan much after that! I went to see Miss MacEwen today. She has been to Guernsey for two or three days and says it is awful, like a dead town, nothing much in the shops, not a single bus of any sort running, only those chairs (or low pony carriages) and nothing under four of five shillings for ever such a little distance. I expect the German chiefs have plenty of petrol for their cars, greedy devils!

August 17th, 1940

What a glorious week of victory we have had, ending today, and now a great calm. I wonder for how long. Even the heavy firing on the French coast has stopped for the time being.

I have been feeling downhearted and depressed. It is being cut off, I think, from all we love, our lack of papers, letters and a hundred and one things that make life bearable. It is wicked to feel like it I know, when so many are suffering and in want. I still go to the Red Cross depot but as no clothing can be sent away we are using the wool and materials to make clothes for the Sark kiddies. There is a great lack of wearing materials and wool in the Islands.

August 20th, 1940

Quite a change in the weather, wintry and cold and our curfew is at 10pm instead of 11pm. We are lucky to have paraffin lamps here, because in Guernsey the water and electricity supplies are nearly exhausted and they are afraid of an epidemic of some sort. Food supplies are getting low too, although I manage to make a dinner out of nothing. We had fried onions, nice and brown, fried tomatoes, boiled potatoes in their jackets, and Sark butter today.

August 23rd, 1940

Another awful Friday. We were awakened at 2.30am. A bomb had been dropped on Sark and it really seemed as if it must have hit Stock's or Dixcart Hotel, the noise was so heavy, and the suspense and worry until we could hear at daylight what had happened, were intense. It is a mercy no fire was started, or it never could have been put out, as there is no water and no appliances of any sort. It fell near the Manoir, all Mrs Cook's block had the glass shattered and holes cut in the roofs everywhere; the old Vicarage, the new one; and Mrs Judkin's house, but no injury or lives lost. We heard last evening the British Government had given the Germans forty days to clear out of the Islands and they are bombing Jersey, Guernsey and Alderney. I don't think the attempt was made for Sark purposely, it may have been a fight while over the Islands, but it was pretty bad while it lasted.

August 26th, 1940

There is hardly a pane of glass unbroken at the Vicarage, and if the bomb had been larger the whole corner at the Manoir would have been wrecked, but the people are all very calm about it, the first bit of real war to come so close. We hear today that Alderney is to be made an air-base for the Germans, and the forty Guernsey men who went over to clear up the Island are to be sent back to Guernsey, so it will be inhabited by Germans only. We seem to be right in the danger line here in Sark as it is a direct course from France and the planes go right over our house. A large piece of shrapnel, 1lb in weight, was picked up in the meadow next to this house after the bomb fell.

August 28th, 1940

We still have the wireless. The north-east coast seems to be having bad raids and I worry about Auntie Betty. I also wonder how you and Collins are. There seems to be no hope of getting our postcards through to our relations on the mainland, another of the German promises broken. I dread the winter coming, the curfew may then be any time after 4 or 5 in the afternoon, (think of it!), until about 7 or 8 in the morning. By then our knitting and sewing will be all finished. I think we must spend half of the time in bed to save all round. The order in the Islands now is that all houses that have been left by evacuees are to have all things taken out and distributed to people in need—clothes, boots, food or any stores whatever, especially coal, oil and wood. Some of the poor people when they return will get a nasty shock, seeing that no one could take anything but hand luggage when they left the Islands.

It is a blessing that all the folk were cleared off Alderney. We hear about one thousand German marines are to be billeted there. The bombing and machine-gunning is terrific here. There cannot be much of Cherbourg left and all the French coast is lit up like fireworks at night. There will not be much left of Northern France soon.

August 30th, 1940

For the first time in one hundred years cattle are to be brought from France to Guernsey and killed for the German troops we are told. Norah goes out fishing and although she does not get much every little helps even if it only feeds the cat. She gets limpets which we scald and cut up for the hens which I am trying my hardest to hang on to but it is very hard to keep feeding them. It is into the third month now since the invasion and I have not seen a German yet and I go out every day.

September 1st, 1940

A glorious summer day and it is twelve months since war was declared. What a lot has happened since then to these peaceful little Islands. I don't think they will ever get prosperous and happy again. The bays and lanes are deserted and there is no excitement of a boat coming to gladden our hearts. There is terrific firing on the sea which sounds like a naval battle and shakes every window in the house. I am glad Berlin is feeling the war a bit, for perhaps if it comes nearer home Hitler will soften his heart and try to mend his ways. I am thinking little Judy will be nearly two months old now. I wonder how old she will be before I see her.

September 4th, 1940

Not much fresh news here, except lots of gun-fire in the Channel. When the French airports are knocked out of action the Government ought to turn their attention to the Channel Islands. The Germans will take some moving from the Isles, they are better treated than ever they have been in their lives I should think. They go bathing in Dixcart Bay every day and even take the Bel Air white blankets on which to sunbathe, living like fighting cocks, eating all our nourishing food. It will be a happy day for us when we wave them goodbye!

In Guernsey it is much worse and they even go to the farms and command them to give over the eggs and fowls. Dr Pittard says we must all bury our potato crops or they will take them, and as this is our mainstay for the winter it would be serious, but I feel we shall be relieved before the winter.

September 8th, 1940

I wonder if I told you that the States of Guernsey are allowing Auntie Annie £10 a month until we can get in touch with the mainland again. It is a big relief to me, although Mrs Babbe offered to keep her for nothing if it had not been agreed upon. They are such kind people and of course it would be paid back in full when victory comes. Oh, what a happy day that will be!

If only the Germans would leave the Islands our lot would not be so bad, and the hardships of the war we would gladly share, and do. The electric light, water supply and sanitary arrangements are going to be serious in Guernsey and as the 1,800 troops, or nearly all, are occupying the best hotels and large houses, even Castle Carey, they will suffer worse for lack of water and light, so perhaps it will shift them sooner than we think, otherwise it may mean an epidemic of some kind.

September 9th, 1940

We ourselves are not doing too badly. I have had to reduce my hens by about half because I cannot get the feeding stuff. We exchange the eggs for butter and bread. Eggs are now about 2s 3d a dozen but the Germans are eating them all up and it is said they get plenty of bacon for breakfast too. We cannot get bacon, cheese or margarine and very little lard, about 1oz a week only, until the stores give out. When the shops are empty that will be the end of the stores. Fortunately I have a store of tea and sugar, coffee, cocoa, Ovaltine, Bengers, malted milk, Quaker oats, oatmeal, flour, rice, peas and beans, Bovril, Oxo cubes, soup squares, macaroni and such like and Mrs Falle lets us have one pint of milk a day, to be paid for when we can. Of course there is a well-stocked vegetable garden and plenty of potatoes, thank God, so I need not tighten my belt yet. We have much to be thankful for.

Did you hear the broadcast appeal for the Channel Isles' refugees last evening? Still our little Sark was not mentioned, so they apparently think we are perfectly safe, and indeed we are and can go to bed and sleep. What an awful raid on London yesterday, poor, dear people, and still it goes on. God only knows what we are in for, it is safe nowhere, how I worry about you all.

It was Harvest Festival in our little church yesterday, and it looked so beautiful that it is very hard to believe there is a war on in almost every country and unrest everywhere. We are rationed for bread this week as the flour is giving out. We are allowed $\frac{3}{4}$lb of bread each a day. Well, we do not eat that amount, it is the mothers with big families that will feel it most, but I believe allowances will be made while white flour lasts. After that, well no one knows, it cannot come from England unless the Red Cross bring it. France may send us some, I wonder.

September 10th, 1940

The Germans are very nicely dug in here but some of them say they will be home in Germany for Christmas, believing they will have won the war, you bet! It is fortunate for us that they are not so unbearable as they appear to be in Guernsey. There they are breaking into the unoccupied houses and stealing—here, I am sorry to say, they mix too freely with the Sark people although no harm seems to have come from it yet, but my intention is to keep clear. Even yet I have not seen them and I go out every day somewhere.

September 11th, 1940

I have been depressed all day but I have a presentiment about all of you. We heard Mr Churchill's speech tonight on the likely invasion by barges, also that a bomb had been dropped outside Buckingham Palace. What a splendid example our King and Queen are to the nation, there is no other country in the world like it.

September 16th, 1940

I must make my Diary weekly now because of paper shortage and while we are German prisoners there is no more to be had. The ten German soldiers who have been here for ten weeks have gone and sixteen more have come in their place, horrid-looking creatures, and we are told the laws are to be tightened up, and if some are broken then it will be the death penalty. Cheerful, isn't it? So this chicken is going to mind her p's and q's, you bet! We wonder if they will get their fat bodies away and how. If the British Navy get round these waters there might be some dirty work with us in the front line, but the Germans are absolute cowards—the minute they know that things are going against them I expect they will flee in wild disorder. Worse and worse, we hear we are to have about thirty more Germans and the Island has to be fortified so they are placing guns everywhere and just taking over any house that suits them. I am thankful we have no sea view.

September 22nd, 1940

We have lots of south-westerly gales and I hope we get lots more to stop the German antics on the sea; no barge could live in these awful seas and it would take a warship all its time. I often wish I were on the mainland doing my bit, it would be better than waiting here. I am having to cut my hens down to about six or eight and try to hold on to them for a few eggs as I cannot get food with which to feed them. We get the German news in our paper and I see the chemical works at Billingham have been bombed, also the North West, Birkenhead and Liverpool. Jersey and Guernsey Airports were well bombed this week.

September 26th, 1940

Here we are again, merry and bright and still hoping for some word from the mainland. Two days ago an English plane dropped leaflets over Guernsey telling us we were not forgotten; also some English papers, together with photos of the King and Queen and Buckingham Palace, so they evidently think we are without the wireless. I am thankful to say we still have that and it is a blessing to hear the news. We hear with grief about the awful raids on London and the loss of life and buildings, especially churches and hospitals. I wonder if we shall ever find each other again. If we could only get an English boat. We hear a yacht got away from Guernsey in a fog with ten men on it bound for England, so we think that is the reason for the leaflets being dropped, telling us to 'cheer up, help will come soon'. Also they said, if they did reach England alive they would give five thousand pounds for a Spitfire and that has been announced on the wireless. Brave men to brave these seas, for some days they are terrific.

Oh, for an English newspaper. We have not seen one since the middle of June, or a *Radio Times*. Everyone is so good to us; it seems every time I go out I bring home a basketful from some hospitable soul and we also exchange what we have most of. We have had to cut out drinking tea because it is not available. We have no fats, bacon, cheese and little wheat. Chicken food goes into the bread to make it up and it is as black as ink, for there is no yeast to be had and no hops, for beer is scarce, consequently the bread is as heavy as lead. Oh, for a bit of home-made Stockton bread.

October 1st, 1940

There is a dismal plane that goes over here every night and keeps patrolling the Islands to see that all our lights are out. There is a rumour that someone is signalling to the enemy, so they are very guarded. It makes a noise like an old cow in distress all night long, worse than the fog horns at the lighthouse. Drastic notices are in every shop window in Guernsey and Sark about sheltering any men who are dropped by parachute (our men), and as a parachute is supposed to have dropped four men last week it looks a bit serious for some of the Guernsey folk. They are supposed to have mingled with the Guernsey people. What object they have in mind we don't know, unless it is to cut the cable to France and Germany.

The German hour is to be taken off this week so instead of being two hours in advance of the clock we will only be one. It has been so misleading for meals, getting up and going to bed, so I shall be glad. With our necessities becoming shorter I think it will be bed and hot water bottles most of the time to save food and oil. I am still holding on to a few hens and hoping each day a boat will come with corn. I have sold a lot and have been very glad of the money even though there is not much we can buy, but one must have a little. I told Miss Watts the other day if we get relief and a boat by Christmas we must go to England even if we have to sell the furniture, always supposing the Germans have left us.

October 7th, 1940

I have been very depressed and off colour for two or three days. The sun shines today and I am feeling much better and want to get busy in the garden and storing vegetables. I still go to the Red Cross depot and do a spot of work most fine afternoons, for we can get so little to sew, or wool to knit for ourselves. I wish I had taken advantage of the offer when you said you knew a cheap place to buy some wool, but who would have thought the Germans would come here and control all our stuff. The food problem in Jersey is much worse than in Guernsey or Sark for last week hens and pullets

35

brought up to 18s each. I have to get mine ready for the oven and only get 2s 6d or 3s. It is a sin to have to kill them all off but there is absolutely no food to be had to keep them alive. I was so proud of the flock and it was a great source of income to us. I did not put down many eggs this year, thinking I would always have new-laid ones in hand.

October 14th, 1940

Nothing very startling has happened this week but we hear that Guernsey is to be bombed again, and leaflets have again been dropped telling the residents to keep away from the airport and the White Rock and that we shall have communication with the mainland sooner than we think. I hope the RAF will take Alderney next and make it an air-base, then this lot might flee. What this war will leave us with I don't know, with our nerves on edge constantly, what will they be like in years to come? I listened to Princess Elizabeth's speech last evening which was splendid. What wonderful people they all are, especially Winston Churchill—*he* is marvellous.

October 21st, 1940

What awful nights you are having in England. My heart goes out to you all and I often wish I had got away from Sark and was able to do a bit more towards the sick and suffering. There is so little we can do here, only watch and wait until we are released, for we are surely German prisoners. The food problem is not as acute as we once thought it would be. For some unknown reason they are bringing stores from France each week, even wheat. I should have thought they would have sent it to Germany. It is most essential that they send us feeding stuff for the animals because if they are killed off, our milk, butter and meat will go. At present we (Norah and I) get ½lb fresh butter a week. (The ration is really only ¼lb.) Some good friend at court! We do miss not getting cheese, for one can make such nice savoury dishes with that. We get good home-killed meat and a decent ration of that. It is money that is so scarce to buy it with. I have no more hens to sell and what I have kept don't lay. They may soon, with a stroke of luck!

Someone has been to Guernsey for the day, and says things are still worse there, as regards food especially. The 1,800 German troops are costing the States £1 a day each, all the bulb industry and glasshouses have to produce food to feed everyone. Meanwhile

36

the Germans are walking about as pleased as punch, like young Hitlers, all in full kit and fully armed, knives down their top-boots, a pistol on each hip, and a loaded gun on the shoulder—the swines. The German film last week was called *Dancing Round the World*, which is exactly what they are doing, trying to put fear into everyone's hearts. Our lot of Germans here in Sark have been changed three times since the Occupation; the last lot were quarrelsome in the public houses (they drink beer by the bucket!) so these are to be fired today and some more take their place, perhaps they will be worse, who knows?

The curfew is now 9pm to 7am, all out after that will be shot, how nice! Last week I dreamt a beautiful white ship arrived in the harbour and I took charge of a child about two years old, but I could not find you anywhere and I did not know if the child was yours.

Mr Churchill's speech last night was to France, it gives one fresh hope. We were very disappointed about the broadcast telling about the Channel Isles. Sark seems to be off the map. I don't know what I expected to hear, perhaps a message from you saying, 'Hello Mum, how are you?', but never a voice. Perhaps they will do it every week and we may hear something soon. The one thing about Sark is we have nearly all stood together and are carrying on very bravely through it all. We don't know what is in store for us, the Germans tighten up the laws each week. It is good to know England has not forgotten us. Dr Pittard says he won't forgive England for letting the Germans have the Channel Isles, but I don't see how it could have been avoided without wholesale slaughter.

October 28th, 1940

Yesterday we were asked out to dinner and spent the day at Dixcart Hotel, one of the ladies there had a birthday. It was really nice and not at all like wartime or being German prisoners. We had champagne as well. Please don't think we live like that every day. Next day was a fast, baked potatoes with butter followed by a cup of coffee. We still look fit and are by no means starving although the Germans have stopped the fishing again and no one is allowed to leave or enter the Island without a special permit, even to Guernsey. This week we have all to fill in registration forms worse than passports, they certainly don't mean us to run away. Since the eight men got away from Guernsey by boat to England they are very anxious it should not happen again.

37

October 31st, 1940

My birthday, and wonder of wonders, although the shops are nearly sold out I had such a lot of presents. Norah it would appear has been raiding the shops for weeks. She bagged the last pair of slippers for me, a tin of malted milk (bedtime tonic) and a warm sleeping coat. My nightgowns that you made me are so patched that none, or hardly any, of the original can be seen, still I am happy and full of hope that help will come. It is a glorious sunshiny morning and who can doubt that 'God is in His heaven'. Oh, more presents: a bottle of brandy (from ladies at Dixcart), two boxes of cigarettes from Auntie Carter, a warm helmet from Mary Watts and a bottle of Guinness Stout, not bad in wartime, is it?

November 6th, 1940

Not much news this week. We are rationed for clothes now and have a book of 100 coupons each that have to be doled out as we require things. Most shops in Guernsey have had to close, no more goods in stock. We are to have thirty more soldiers sent over and we hear that they are to be billeted at Stock's Hotel. I hate to feel they are so close. Some say they will be Marines and not too bad. Those staying at the Bel Air are a mad lot, not fit to be about. I have been seedy for a week and am not feeling too good.

November 16th, 1940

The German soldiers have left the Bel Air Headquarters (the rain pours in everywhere). They have gone to the Manoir (the old Vicarage) seventeen or eighteen of them, fancy to mess up a lovely house like that! Eighteen more are stationed at Stock's Hotel and it is known they are Gestapo men, so we are near enough and afraid to breathe. It is strange but we hardly know what is going on, even on this little Island. We have all to have permits to go to Guernsey and to come back, searching questions are being asked even of the oldest residents, such rot! We hear, and think it is true, that the German soldiers are rebelling in Guernsey and that nine have been shot and a special lot of Police sent from France to keep guard, poor devils, no wonder, as they were told they were being sent to the Isle of Wight, and being so near England they thought all would be over by Christmas and they would be back in Germany.

November 20th, 1940

Oh, day of mourning! They have taken our wirelesses away and we are cut off from everything. There is only the Guernsey rag of a paper and that in time will be all German news. In Guernsey they have changed the names of streets to German, lessons in German are taken and given everywhere, and our identity cards, received this week, are printed in German with the eagle and swastika on, what nice souvenirs they will be after the war! A huge plane was brought down at Brecqhou last week by one of our planes and it has lifted the roof off the house and broken every window, but no one was in residence. It passed right over this house in flames and the report was awful. I quite thought half Sark was wiped out.

One hundred and eighty wirelesses were handed in to the Germans. Mrs Hathaway has written to Headquarters asking for us to have them back soon, but rumour says there is a transmitter somewhere on the Islands and they are, I suppose, trying to track it down. I hope they don't find it, but I do hope we get the wireless back again, it is miserable to be cut off from all news from home and not to know how the war is going on. The propaganda in their news makes you think *they* are on the winning side and that makes me very down hearted at times. It is not light until 10am, for we have English summer time and one hour German as well, so it seems all night and no day. The paraffin is giving out and we are only allowed one candle a week so we mostly sit by firelight. The lighthouse has been taken over by the German Marines so the store of paraffin there is being used by them. I mostly go to bed in the dark, I am all bruises and bumps. The fishermen have not to go out until 11am and then accompanied by two or three Germans. They have all had their photos taken and have to show them going out and coming in, did you ever hear of such rot!

Old Bill Hamon asked one of the Huns if he thought his face could change in two or three hours! They say there is a shortage of paper, but if you could see the notices and papers they can distribute on trivial matters it certainly does not look like it. The provisions hold out fairly well, but Stock's cows got into the garden one day and made a good meal of it.

December 7th, 1940

No wireless back yet and it is pretty lonely. Needless to say there are countless rumours and we don't know what to believe. What we hear one day is denied the next. It is said all German women have been called back to Germany from Guernsey and Jersey. There were masses of them, typists for the telegraph and telephones, and nurses and doctors. Our poor sick and wounded have to go over to Castel. There were over 2,000 German soldiers in Guernsey at first but 500 or 800 have been sent back, so perhaps they are beginning to see they might be cut off. The storms we have had and are still having are alarming. It is a great wonder our houses stand up to it. I don't envy those on duty at this harbour in the south-west gales, all night long. They are looking out for submarines. Several are supposed to have come to Guernsey and the men actually landed, so no wonder they are getting uneasy and want to depart. I would like to see them cut off.

No Stockton plum cake this year. I have been saving my butter for weeks to try to make a small cake for the festive time and we all mean to make ourselves as happy as we can, we have a lot to be thankful for.

December 14th, 1940

Great joy, we have the wireless back and it makes life much easier to know what is going on across the seas.

Christmas is not far off now and I still hope for a letter from someone, even a postcard. Some have come through the Red Cross. We have been invited to the Dixcart Hotel for Christmas Day, a party of seven or eight of us, so it will be nice for us as we have no fatted calf to kill this Christmas. I have not even made a pudding so I cannot give a dinner party, it must be tea parties for return visits. Somehow we don't seem to get the Christmas spirit this year with these horrid Germans about and they *are* loathsome, especially the lot at Stock's Hotel. We long for the British Navy to come and put the fear of God in their hearts, and I pray it won't be far off. The firing on the French coast is terrific sometimes, it will only be when they have driven them out of Northern France that our relief will come.

December 25th, 1940

We feel ever so gay, have both been to church and are looking forward to a nice party at Dixcart Hotel.

What a strange Christmas, no news from any of my dear ones and not a glimpse of hope. I cannot enter into the Christmas feeling at all. Who would have thought we could have been cut off like this, German prisoners.

December 26th, 1940

We spent a very happy day and had a good dinner of roast beef (home-killed) and Yorkshire pudding, Brussels sprouts, plum pudding, mince pies and champagne galore. We heard the King's speech and drank his health in port wine, then we played games and nice prizes were given. Needless to say, I got the booby prize, but it is quite a useful one. As our curfew is 10pm we all made a start for home at 9.30 after a very happy day, so I hope you have not been worrying about us and perhaps thinking we had no Christmas dinner. Things are not as bad as that and I do not think we shall get starved out. They are battering the northern ports so heavily that all the Germans are getting scared and dread being made prisoners.

On Boxing Day we went to Mary Watts's to dine, so you see how I am saving my cupboard! On Sunday we are asked out and again the following week and on Wednesday of this week I am going to see Mr and Mrs Toplis to have tea there.

New Year's Eve

We did not wait to see the New Year in but were awakened at 12 by the reports of gun-firing. Norah came in to my room scared but Mum said, 'It's all right, the Navy has come', but it proved otherwise the Germans at Stock's Hotel had a drop too much and started firing to let the New Year in. They are a mad lot and it is not safe to be about after dark. I am afraid Gabby will be trotted off to France if she does not keep her tongue quiet, she hates the Germans so much and says all sorts about Hitler and Goering quite openly. She has been warned and Mrs Falle is very worried about her and so is poor Bert.

January 1st, 1941

A happy New Year to you all in dear old England. However much it is being bombed it is not so isolated as being here and fearing the worst. All we can do is to put our trust in God for an early victory. It is hard not seeing a newspaper but a great blessing we got our wireless back, although soon that will be no use because there are no more dry batteries to be had in any of the Islands and it is hardly likely they will bring any from France.

We are still getting enough to eat; tea we hear has quite given out, but *we* have a few packets left, also several pounds of coffee. We get plenty of pork but there is no more beef to kill so when the pigs give out it will be Oxo cubes and soup from cabbage water. I have been careful and thrifty all my life but this is 'larning me' a bit more! I kept twelve pullets and am trying hard to feed them so as to have eggs soon, but there is no corn to be had. It is very cold and wintry today and we have had hailstones as big as maize, so the little blighters are mopping it up like mad thinking it is corn. It is funny to see them!

January 11th, 1941

Nothing much has happened since the first, except the Germans are taking photos of the whole Island for a film to be shown in Berlin. When I saw them standing at our gate I felt they might ask me to stand at the front door to complete the picture, but happily they passed on to Stock's Hotel. The German Sergeant asked Mr Remphrie if he would walk past their Headquarters with Mrs Remphrie leading the cows and saluting as they passed. Poor old man, he was a little scared, but considered for a bit, then said, 'Am I obliged to do it?' 'No,' said the German, 'but we would like to make a nice picture.' Then says the old man, 'Will you please tell me what it is for?' The German replied that they were making a film of Sark and the people to be shown in Germany because the Sark people had given no trouble and been very kind. Mr Remphrie replied, 'Then I have no wish to be photographed.'

They have started to patrol the Island now, and two or three were parading in this lane the other day with loaded guns and all complete. It is they who are eating up all our food, tobacco, eggs, cigarettes and all wine and spirits. They don't like beer. We are rationed for cigarettes and tobacco now and there are no sweets of any kind and no fruit and chocolate, it is a great miss and so strange to see all the sweet bottles empty. There is no sewing cotton or darning wool, so soon we shall be clothed in the wild rhubarb leaves that grow so big in Dixcart Valley! One thing we are very rich in, that is plenty of wood and we have nice warm fires. Coal is nearly £5 a ton, therefore we cannot buy that. The Germans are buying up all the tinned food to send home to Germany. They each send 11lb a week home, so all our salmon and sardines are going that way. Thank God the spring is coming!

January 19th, 1941

The days are getting a bit longer, it is light until nearly 8 in the evening, so we are saving oil and candles. To get two candles a week we have to get a permit from Guernsey. We get $\frac{1}{2}$lb of flour a week. We listen anxiously to the announcements on the wireless and are always hoping to have a message from England. We hear from the invaders that we are to be given back to France after the war and they have even begun to arrange and reconstruct the Islands. They say when everyone left Alderney the French people came over and took all the furniture and all valuables and all these poor evacuees are cheerfully waiting the day to return home.

January 27th, 1941

It is more than a week since I scribbled but so little seems to happen at present. We have received some messages through the Red Cross but they are not of much comfort because some of them are dated August 1940. It appears we can send fifteen words back in reply.

The rules are being tightened up more for it seems a naval boat out near L'Ancresse sent a pinnace ashore and shot the sentry and took four guards prisoner, so it makes it hard for us all. Fancy January nearly out already and we shall have been isolated nearly eight months. I thought at the time it would have only been a few weeks, that is why I started a daily diary, now paper is so short I don't know if I will be able to keep on. The shops are only going to open twice a week to give the rations out which are very few and meagre. No jam or marmalade is to be had so we have oatmeal for breakfast, vegetable soup of all kinds for lunch, hardly any meat. When out shooting rabbits last week, one German shot his pal, fifteen bullets in the thigh, and he had to have a special boat to Guernsey to have them extracted. I wish the Germans were not so near us. Happy the day when they depart. Oh, let it be soon!

February 1st, 1941

We have had heavy snow this week and it is so cold and bleak. Things have been very quiet here for two or three weeks, no planes, no firing of guns and one begins to wonder what it all means. I hope the invasion stunt is all off and it only means they are short of material.

February 14th, 1941, St Valentine's Day

We all wonder very much if we shall be here in a trap another winter, if so we shall certainly have wasp waists. I have reduced six or eight inches on the hips already and tightened the belt considerably. I expect very soon everything will give out at the shops, there is a mad rush there as soon as they are open, but the stocks are very low. There are only a few tins of fruit that we jolly well can't afford. Flour still holds out, a little oatmeal left, potatoes nearly all used and you know how the Sark people like them. The butcher says today there will be a few more pigs to kill for a week or two, then . . . but we are all cheerful and still expecting the Good Old British Navy.

February 18th, 1941

The Germans still continue to eat all our stores, great fat, ugly, dissipated hounds. I feel I would like to stab them in the back, they are all bursting out of their clothes with such good living. We have hardly any more clothes in the shops but they send huge parcels every week to the womenfolk in Germany; vests, stockings, wool frocks, shoes and every available thing, so we come second and get nothing. The shopkeepers started to hide things under the counter, but the 'pigs' go right behind and fish them out. They buy up all the soap and Lux. Happy day for us when they go. I know I shall get drunk that day and I know a few others who will too.

It was Miss MacEwan's birthday yesterday, she was very bucked, she had a letter from her sister. The weather is not so cold, so we need less firing. I cannot afford coal, it is nearly five shillings a cwt. We are thankful for the wood we can cut down and burn. The spring flowers are pushing up and everywhere tells of spring and summer ahead, and please God—peace.

I am reduced to reading papers that are dated 1912 and find them quite interesting, they came out of Mrs Judkin's house, she has hoarded for years. No one has papers to light for fires or for anything.

March 1st, 1941

Here we are into another month. If anyone had told me last June we would have our unwelcome guests for eight or nine months I should have called them liars, and here we are each week getting more short of food, not luxuries but necessities.

There won't be a shortage of water on Sark for the duration as it has rained steadily for three months. But at least it stays light until 9pm so we go to bed in the daylight. Hardly any planes go over at all, except when they bomb Guernsey Airport, then it is pretty lively. I don't think Hitler will invade England, he means to do something greater to try and put old Mussolini in favour if it is possible.

The postage stamps in Guernsey are giving out and they are to issue new ones. They will be historical won't they? Also they have cut the twopenny stamps in half for penny postage.

There are just as many troops in Guernsey and Sark, all lazing about, having fights and getting drunk. We have had no trouble yet except for one night when they walked down the front gravel path about 2 or 3 in the morning, but it was apparently part of their patrol. Dr Pittard said, 'Why didn't you put your head out of the window and say, "What the hell do you want at this time?"', but my idea is to say as little as possible to the brutes, get indoors at curfew time, and give them no chance to insult you. Then look what Hitler has trained them to be—a foul, fat, ugly, bullet-headed lot, capable of doing any dirty deed. They drink all day and all night. My surest wish for them is that they could see a few Sark ghosts, the monk or the lady in white—that might sober them. They do no drill of any kind, just strut along the lanes armed to the teeth with their behinds bursting out of their breeches with such good living. This coming week there are no cigarettes or tobacco for anyone. Only for the German troops, that is enough to make the Sark men see red to take away their smokes.

March 4th, 1941

Red Cross day and a red letter day for us! I am delighted and so is Norah with your news of Judith Margaret's arrival. She will now be nearly nine months old and by the time I see her she will be walking and talking I expect. The message gave address as only Bath, so we take it you have been evacuated there. I am so glad. Where is Collins and his people? Eric's message gave no address, just 'anxious for news' and asking if we can reply. Well, we can and the message is being sent from here on Saturday 8th March. We are told it will take seven or eight weeks, so it will be April or probably May before you receive it. What a long time to wait for your answer. By then, who knows what may happen, we may be free. Oh, if only these devils would go back to where they belong. I never thought I should live to see through three wars and then be a German prisoner. Curse 'em.

Ho ho, and a bottle of rum, Mrs Falle (from Stock's) came into us and brought us some books to read and a bottle of rum for me to have in my hot milk at night, so I drank Judith's health in rum.

The food controller has been over from Guernsey to look around and see what we have. All available land has to be cultivated and hundreds of tons of potatoes planted and if Sark can send tons of potatoes to Guernsey they will send us provisions in return. I am soling my boots with those rubber mats that come off pub counters and have 'Pony Ales' and 'Guinness Stout' written on them, so I must be careful when I kneel not to show my soles! The mats are grass green in colour and the writing is in white, quite posh, I tell you. As for stockings, well, the less said about these the better; Norah is trying to hold together with the help of ankle socks, (I pinched the wool) but *I* have to *face* all my friends when out and never let them get behind me.

We were getting quite a lot of provisions from France until a week or two ago and strange to say we were having Nestlés milk with 'for the forces' printed on it. We also had Australian butter, very good too. We think they are some of the provisions our men had to leave behind. I got weighed today at Mrs Durand's and I have lost one stone seven pounds since I saw you last and I feel all the better for it, but I don't want to get too thin or I shall be scraggy. Norah longs for a bit of cheese, it seems a great need for her. Sometimes we get a small box of Camembert from France and the smell is too awful, it tastes all right, but the last box we really had to give away, it was the limit, it smelt just like a corpse in the house. We gave it to Mary Watts and she just revelled in it.

I have been stopped and congratulated hundreds of times about the arrival of Judith Margaret, everyone in Sark knows her name and knew the message before I got it. Old Mr and Mrs Cook were so pleased to hear, so were the Toplises, Mrs Campbell, Miss Cheesewright, Miss Watts and Howard and Miss Carter and lots more, too numerous to mention.

March 15th, 1941

Another message from you, Collins and Judith to say all is well. We are frantically planting our gardens with all sorts of good things for the coming winter, but God forbid we should have another winter as German prisoners. Our bread ration is to be reduced this week, so it will be an entirely potato diet soon and not even the herrings to go with it. The Germans have put a ban on fishing. About once a month we get one ounce of Guernsey sweets, six in number, think of it! No chocolate, no jam or fruit of any kind, not even an orange or a lemon. It is a great miss, no currants, raisins, rice, oatmeal or any pudding stuffs. We often feel empty so God help us if we have to face another winter.

March 25th, 1941

Norah has been to Dixcart Bay for limpets to feed the hens. If the eggs taste of fish we shall have an extra course thrown in! Mrs Cook and John Henry are eating limpets and enjoy them. I would sooner eat cat's flesh, it would taste a bit like rabbit.

Poor Miss MacEwan was in today and she was saying how bare her cupboard was and she asked me if she could make a good pot of soup from the water a cauliflower had been boiled in. I said, put in some lentils, split peas or barley to give it flavour, but she had not got an ounce of anything in the house, and that is how we are going on. All the gorseland is being cultivated, anyone can cut it by arrangement. The good old brick ovens are being used again, and the bread is delicious, so if enough wheat can be grown I don't see how we can starve.

April 11th, 1941, Good Friday

We are now permitted to write twenty-five words in our messages to the mainland to the Red Cross, but we have to be so guarded in what we say, I expect they are heavily censored. Things are getting pretty bad, for the Germans are taking all our nourishing food. I thank God I kept one dozen hens and they are laying about six eggs a day. I can only feed them on house scraps and potato peelings but the eggs are worth gold here. The Germans are sending all our new-laid eggs to Germany. We have to hide the new eggs each day because they have a house-to-house search.

Easter Sunday

A beautiful sunny day and the primroses are out everywhere, and the daffodils. Norah has been busy decorating the church and it looks lovely. She has had a very bad cold (the first this winter). I expect we are just beginning to feel the pinch a bit. Poor Auntie Annie has had a stroke, the Doctor says she may go at any time. I cannot go over to see her, because it is only German boats that ply backwards and forwards to Guernsey from Sark and they all have

47

the swastika on and so are liable to be fired on by any of our planes overhead. Some of the Sark folk venture but I want to live a bit longer to see Judith Margaret.

April 14th, 1941

The Germans are calling all the English silver coins in on the Islands so the States of Guernsey are issuing 2s 6d and 5s notes. Poor, poor Guernsey is in an awful state by all accounts, nearly every shop closed and those that are open only have an odd bottle or two of furniture cream and a few boxes of matches in the windows. That nice big store 'Le Riche' is quite empty, so is Collin's and the Guernsey Sweet Shop and Woolworth's. There is no tea at all and coffee is being made from all sorts of things—parsnips cut in pieces and roasted in the oven, then ground, and called Parffee. Barley done the same way is called Barffee then there is dandelion coffee (roots roasted). The only thing we get unadulterated seems to be potatoes, and we eat them fried for breakfast, boiled for dinner and sometimes, to help the bread out, potato cakes for tea, and fried for supper, if there are any left over. Strange to say I am not getting fat on it. Our biggest miss is the tea and sugar ration, that is giving out altogether. Poor Miss MacEwan was in again today, looking very miserable, she said she had not had a cup of tea for a week or ten days, and as you know, all her brothers and brother-in-law are in the tea trade so she always has a case at a time and the poor soul is feeling it very badly. I had a nice wee bit and quickly got the kettle boiling. I also gave her two teaspoonfuls for her tea in the morning and she went off in high spirits. She has had a Red Cross message from her brother in Scotland asking if she is in want of food, clothes or money. We have had seven messages but no one has asked *us* and there is no one poorer in Sark. I don't suppose if we did ask for anything we should get it by the Red Cross. One message we had was from some friends, real nice guests, who have stayed with us four or five years during the summer.

April 23rd, 1941

It seems dreadful to think that a peaceful little Isle like this could be turned into a Hitler village. The walls are all posted with notices about what we are not to do, and it all ends with death penalties, even if we are found talking about Germans. One Guernsey man has been put in prison for saying, 'I wish a few Spitfires would come and settle them.' He was just referring to some German planes flying over. He was tapped on the shoulder and taken off. Some of the Sark girls are walking out with the German soldiers, silly little asses, I feel I would like to shake them.

April 26th, 1941 (Norah's birthday)

We had some fat washed up in one of the bays and have been allowed $\frac{1}{4}$lb each. It is just like tallow or candle fat and is as hard as a rock. I shall try and make a birthday cake for Norah with it. The food problem will become worse because 2,000 more Germans have been sent to Guernsey from Cherbourg. They say they have been bombed out there. After this week we are told there will be no more meat for some weeks, unless someone produces an underfed pig.

May 1st, 1941

The weather is bitterly cold and we have had a severe frost which has nipped some people's potatoes. The garden is becoming kfficult to manage, we cannot afford labour and I keep saying I hope my next house will only have a window box, God knows where the next house will be, I hope not France or Germany. We are nearly shaken out of our beds with all the firing at Cherbourg and Brest and the activity at night, starting every time at about 11pm. It is awful. We have the curfew until 11pm now and it is almost daylight then. Two hundred pounds of chocolate have been purchased by the States of Guernsey for the children only, up to sixteen years of age, so Sark has had its portion this week. The children need it, they begin to look very weedy. We have got to provide the German troops with 15doz new-laid eggs a week, they demand it. We get a few, but I hide them, it will be sure death if I am caught.

May 10th, 1941

The harbour works have had to close for want of cement and materials. Fifteen of the men have gone to Alderney to do the harbour repairs there. Poor devils, they will be near enough to Cherbourg with all its blasting.

I hope I won't have to burn my Diary but I certainly will if there is a house-to-house search.

May 13th, 1941

Today we hear that Hitler's deputy and right hand man has arrived in Scotland by plane. What a dramatic thing to happen and one that was never expected, but it is too soon yet to even guess what may happen, although I like to think there will be other splits in their Government soon.

The Sark folk are just as happy-go-lucky as ever, they have planted more and are using a bit more energy, but of late years they have earned money so easily that hard work is a hardship. Also they are so ignorant but they are to be easily excused, as they have not travelled further than into Guernsey in peace-time, and England or Britain to them is a remote place on the map, if they ever notice it. Their main idea of England is the mail-boat from there every day bringing a lot of provisions and hundreds of visitors. I wish a ship would come with some shoes and stockings and other things too numerous to mention. Wool is 1s 6d an ounce now, so my knitting days are over for a bit. We have had a long cold spring, the coldest I can remember. How the daffodils and primroses can bloom, I don't know. The apple blossom shows signs of a good crop and how we will welcome them. I hope we get some extra sugar for jam. I ought to do some digging of new potatoes next week with a stroke of luck and peas and beans will be along soon after that. Salads too are coming along quickly.

There is a rumour that if we can only stick it three or four months longer, all will be well.

June 1st, 1941

We are now into the twelfth month of the invasion and it has seemed like an eternity. I wonder for how much longer. Little Judith will soon be one year old and I wonder what and who she is like. I also wonder if you are all in your own homes. We have no newspapers and hear so little news. The German troops are holding on tight to these little Islands. They have a lot of parachutists in Guernsey and they are practising invasion off Brecqhou Island, getting ready for invading England, maybe. We hear today on the wireless the two dirty dogs have met again on the Bremar Pass, to plan some more villainy, you bet, but the news is good from America. One day I was passing their Headquarters and heard the Germans listening to Roosevelt's momentous speech, and they are not supposed to listen to English broadcasts, so that tells a story. This lot of troops look very down and dissatisfied with life, one threatened to cut his throat in the Dixcart Bay! It seems as if they are tired of life.

June 12th, 1941

Dear old Mrs Cook was buried last week, I have known her for thirty-four years. The old man is very downhearted, they have lived together in that cottage for over sixty years. Now the cottage is to be given up and he will live with his daughter at La Tour.

The body of a poor Dutchman was washed up in Victor Hugo's cave last week and the Sark people gave him quite a nice funeral on Sunday, nearly all the Sark people attended and the coffin was a mass of lovely flowers and wreaths. I wonder we do not get more wreckage or bodies washed up, but there is very little considering the loss of ships. The Cumbers, (Connie and her mother) are staying at the Dixcart Hotel for two weeks, so we hear all the Guernsey news. I have never known so many deaths and suicides in the Islands, largely amongst men, because all the children and wives who could get away did so. It must be a very lonely life and in Alderney, poor little Isle, the conditions are deplorable, the beautiful houses and farms are stripped.

The Sark men who signed on for five months to do harbour repairs there are all pretending to be sick and getting sent back here. The food is poor and the work hard, only two or three slices of bread a day is allowed to each plus the fish they *can* catch, although the Germans take nearly all.

Here they are practising machine-gunning in Stock's meadow and they take huge guns down to Dixcart Bay and fire out to sea, so imagine the din and noise on this peaceful little Island. It is full of lovely flowers and blossoms, wild and cultivated, and the birds are more plentiful and sing louder each year. The cuckoo is really noisy, and we have got more or less used to the German troops. Sark is not much altered, we each do our gardens and all try to outdo the other for early crops.

Today is washing day and the soap is very scarce. In Guernsey all the laundries have had to close down because of lack of materials and the boot, shoe and stocking problem is most acute. We are both very badly off in this respect.

Permits have to be obtained from the German Commandant to lop trees, cut gorse and for any fuel, but as no trees are allowed to be cut down we are all in a very cold state. We certainly are between the devil and the deep blue sea. It is like being on board a big ship in mid-ocean and the cold is terrific. We get our bread twice a week and most of the children are kept in bed the last day, before receiving it, so that those working can have their share to go to work.

Someone is offering 75s for 1lb of tea this week in the Exchange column. I have had to sell yours and Collins's tennis rackets this week and I am trying to sell the ukulele, all this to buy some seeds and food for the hens, some day I will repay you for them. All the Island people are eating stale vegetables and limpets, no one may go to the bays in ormering tides, it is so heavily mined. There are a thousand Spaniards (labour gang) in Guernsey, all the Frenchmen rebelled and have been sent back. What does seem strange is the Sark divers (those working at the new harbour) have been sent to Guernsey to raise a big ship that was sunk by our planes in the harbour. They had to go almost at the point of the pistol.

July 1st, 1941

It is just one year since we were made prisoners and it seems we have come to grow so used to it. Looking back, the dark blackout days of the long winter are all forgotten in the long summer, sunny days.

I do really feel in my bones that we shall have a boat from England soon. The old witch in Guernsey says, 'We are to have all the evacuated people home by Christmas', and if that is true I will return in the boat they come in and eat my Christmas dinner in England. Strange to say, half our German troops have left the Island, and talk says 'gone to help in Russia'. I say, 'God help them' (the Germans). The last batch to arrive were such a poor unhealthy lot and we are all glad they have gone. There are still about twelve at Stock's but they are police. Everyone in Guernsey has been photographed so that the pictures can be stuck on the identity cards, and we in Sark all have to be done on Tuesday next. I feel like putting my finger to my nose just as the camera clicks. What fun! There have been a lot of restrictions in Guernsey because people have been putting the 'V' sign everywhere. As an overall punishment the bread ration is to be cut down again and it is already too little. Some of the people are really hungry in Sark as well, and the curfew hour is to be 6pm so unless the culprits can be found in seventy hours we are all in for it. I took a pencil out with me the other day to make a lot of Vs on the Mill Studio, but the thought of a concentration camp, at my time of life, checked me.

Last night, in bright moonlight, they bombed the airports at Guernsey and the guns at Brest and Cherbourg shook this house. The bombing is almost hourly now, night and day. Yesterday I hear there was a ton of mail for us waiting at Granville that the Germans won't ship for us, dirty dogs!

July 9th, 1941

We have all been photographed today. I really believe if we were prisoners long enough they would even watch over our sleeping to see that we don't exceed the ration and have less hours to work. There are rules and instructions for everything we do. The latest about the fishermen is that if they want to go out to fish at all they must each put down a £10 deposit and give their word of honour that they won't try to get away and an armed guard is to go with them. Some are bringing up their boats altogether, they have not £10 to put down, seeing none of us have earned any money for two years. Talk says there is a large troop ship in Guernsey Harbour with steam up night and day, and the German troops will get twenty-four hours' notice to board it. Please God, it is not far off.

They have brought three or four tanks to Guernsey, just to show off, and they are racing all over the quaint little town like a lot of mad things, together with motor bikes, all fully armed to the teeth and wearing tin hats. They want to put the fear of God into us I suppose but it had no effect, either here or there. We are keeping a stiff upper lip and carrying on as best we can, but I do wish the BBC would mention us sometimes for we are all trying hard and this wearying waiting is a great strain, especially on us older ones. I have been very seedy for weeks, feeling like a washed-out rag. I think it is the bread we are eating, it is quite sour and as black as ink. There seems to be a mixture of ground beans, bran and soot combined—not too good for old folks' tummies! We get one box of matches a week and about one ounce of salt each. They are obliged to get salt from salt water in Guernsey and Jersey.

Lovells and Fuzzeys do hardly any of their work in the furnishing line, all they seem to use their vans for is to empty and strip houses that have been evacuated and take all beds and mattresses to German Headquarters by German orders. My heart aches for the people that will return one day and the sight that will greet them.

We had another Red Cross message from G. Toplis, which had taken twelve months to come, dated July, 1940, so it bears out what I said about the Germans keeping it waiting at Granville. Soon, I expect, we shall get no more things from France via Granville for the harbour and the train service are so badly bombed there will be no means of transit. Up until now France has supplied us with a lot of things in return for goods and articles taken from these Islands, so we are sure to feel a big draught soon.

July 28th, 1941

The bombing in Guernsey and Jersey is very alarming at times and we hear that more leaflets have been dropped telling the Germans if they don't clear out in a month, they will be bombed out, but the dirty cowards know quite well the civilian population won't be bombed by the British. They are therefore sending for thousands more German troops from France to hide in the Islands, while there are already 14,000 in Guernsey alone living off the fat of the land. We are drying blackberry leaves for tea and grating and drying carrots for coffee. The tobacco is so short that the men are drying dock leaves and coltsfoot and making a mixture of that. The poor fishermen who put down £10 are told they will get it back at the end of the war.

August 3rd, 1941

We are all beginning to get a bit nervy and edgy as things begin to get a little bit more scarce each week and naturally we begin to think of the winter, if we are still prisoners.

Mrs Hathaway heard by a Red Cross message this week that her eldest son had been killed flying, the one who would have inherited. Our wireless has given out at last, so I hear no news and it is somewhat lonely. We hear all the terrific firing in France and it only seems about two miles away for the house shakes so. I hope the transmitter that the Germans cannot find in Guernsey gives daily accounts of all our doings and keeps those in England up to date with all the German devilry. The German Captain here at Stocks actually said he takes his hat off to the man who transmits in Guernsey and after the war would like to shake hands with him!

The Germans' three films this week were *Seven Years' Bad Luck*, *Bismarck* and *The Rothschilds*. I expect Hitler chose them to impress the Guernsey people. We heard today from some people who have been staying in Guernsey that a family of eight had one sheep's heart only for a full week's meat ration. Stocks killed a calf this week and Mrs Falle sent me a little bit of liver. Looking in my Diary on this day last year I see there were only 800 Germans in Guernsey, now today there are 15,000 of them, all feeding on Island butter, milk and cream. Mr Greenhow (our old Vicar) and his wife are here, so we get all the latest Guernsey news from them. Every cottage and house there seems to have soldiers billeted on it. A lot of the Germans, as they were being shipped on their way to fight in Russia, committed suicide on the White Rock, poor devils. I feel very sorry for them. I think the reason so many are being sent to Guernsey is 'things are being made so hot for them in Northern France', also a lot of invalided ones are being sent to the Islands to be nursed up. Hundreds of horses are being landed at Guernsey from Belgium, as oil and petrol is so scarce. Also tons of timber are arriving there to make huts for the soldiers. The Guernsey residents are only allowed $\frac{1}{2}$ pint of skimmed milk a day, about four slices of bread each and fish every third week. Hardly any meat, so God help them all this winter if no relief comes.

August 20th, 1941

Norah has gone to Guernsey to have some teeth out, so I am all on my own. She is staying at Mrs Plummer's (the owner of Maison Carre), they are very simple kind people. I am longing to hear her news when she comes back on Saturday, for I believe Guernsey looks like a wrecked city. She had quite a morning's work to get a permit to go to Guernsey. You never heard such a performance, and to come back it will be the same.

Last week, when some German troops were to be shipped from the White Rock, bound for Russia, they began to mutiny and stoned the officers. The offenders that were caught were punished by having to walk barefoot for hours at a time, right to Vazon, until their feet were bleeding. The others were rammed on the ship and all disarmed in case of rioting. The Germans are bringing Frenchmen and Belgians over to work on a new road, to run from the White Rock out to the airport. All houses, crops or glasshouses in the way are ruthlessly pulled down, all their methods seem to be destructive everywhere. Some of the Sark men who are working at Alderney breakwater were over for a holiday last week and they said it was heartbreaking to see the wrecked houses and the destruction over there. The things they have no use for are all collected on the beach and petrol is poured over them and they are burned. The man who told me said most lovely things were treated in this way, antiques of all sorts. They just keep actual beds, chairs and so on because there are no inhabitants, but I do know there were some lovely homes there before the war and some very wealthy people.

Another notice up this week says, 'Two Frenchmen have been shot for trying to send messages to England by pigeons', and if we do so it is the death penalty here. Also if we aid or help any airmen who happen to come down, likewise. Just fancy, it might easily be one of our own and someone we know, it's awful.

A big porpoise has been caught in one of the fishermen's nets, nine feet long, and it is being cut up in the Guernsey market for food. They say it is just like tunny fish, but *I* won't eat it.

Norah is not back yet, she only went for two or three days but the weather has been very rough and the boats are so small going to and fro to Guernsey, it has been very unsafe.

September 3rd, 1941

Norah came back yesterday, she stayed two weeks, so we can now get full details of the hardships in Guernsey. They are well on the way to starvation. She says it is pathetic to see the hungry faces of the people waiting in the queues for rations, and these include even some of the old Colonels resident in Guernsey and well-to-do people. There are guns mounted everywhere, all round the coast. The Elizabeth College, the Ladies' College and all big places are filled with German troops. All the schools, chapels and halls are fitted with bunks, one on top of the other. This week every unoccupied house is being stripped of its carpets and furniture and these are being packed and shipped to Germany. All the guns, privately owned, have been collected and sent away. The poor Sark men are distressed about this, it will be hard to get new ones after the war. The Island is infested with rats and rabbits, they are eating all the crops.

There is a court case in Sark this week, because a man won't supply the German troops with new-laid eggs. On Monday, Norah was on Gouliot top and saw a real bit of the battle in the Channel. Fifty-nine of our planes came over and bombed four or five heavily-laden barges going to Guernsey with more guns and ammunition. They also bombed the airport for hours.

September 13th, 1941

The latest order in Guernsey is that the old people don't need extra food as they are no more any use to the States, so I suppose they think the sooner they die the better. At all the cinemas and concerts the Germans have first choice of seats, and when the troops are all seated then the Guernsey people can have what is left! Also the army vans and wagons draw up to the market and shops and take all they want before the Guernsey people. There are Germans in the Post Office, the Press Office and *Star* Offices overlooking everything and everybody, nothing is private any more. People are afraid to speak in the streets, the Gestapo is everywhere, two and three abreast. You would laugh heartily if you could see the Exchange column in the Press. One lady would exchange two pairs of pure silk stockings for 2lb sugar, Sunlight soap for $\frac{1}{2}$lb tea, cigarettes for a packet of Quaker oats and so on. We have no tea at all, only what we can make with blackberry leaves, and coffee with dried parsnips, no flour, no cheese, no bacon, and eggs are luxuries. I am still hoping to hang on to my few hens, they have laid well and have been a great benefit to us.

We are all gathering blackberries like mad. I have no sugar, but mean to bottle them and trust to luck and a speedy release from prison to turn them into jam. We had another message from you on Saturday. It is so comforting to get them. By now Judith will be walking and talking. Your message says she is crawling on the floor. Tell her about her Granny and Aunt Norah.

Our new names are Frau Julie Tremayne and Fraulein Norah! They sound nice, don't you think? On Norah's passport to go to Guernsey they have put she was born in Sark, actually she was born in Stockton-on-Tees.

A mine bomb exploded the other night in Dixcart Bay, it was rather alarming. Mr Falle came along to see if we were nervous. I thought it was another bomb on Little Sark.

We are to have no paraffin this winter and there are very few candles left, so how shall we pass the long winter evenings when it gets dark at 5pm? Some people suggest bed and a hot-water bottle. We shall all get sleeping sickness with being in bed so long! The bread gets blacker and blacker. Lanyon says there is every bean and seed imaginable ground up into the flour, grubs included. Soon nothing but a dose of gunpowder will make it rise—yeast is hopeless.

September 21st, 1941

A most gorgeous day, perfect blue sky and not a sound, only the crying of the seagulls and the gentle lapping of the sea. The garden is full of autumn flowers and we have a beautiful bowl of roses on the table. The myrtle bush in front of the drawing-room window is white with blossom, so unusual at this time of year and the scent is delicious when we open the window. The creepers have nearly all died on the house, we cannot think why, unless it is German blight, small wonder, the blighters. The harvest is over and safely in. I have never known such beautiful weather in September. The church looked lovely at the Harvest Festival and was full of all sorts of good things, which were sold afterwards and the money given to the Red Cross and Shipwrecked Men.

Last week a plane (English) came so low over Guernsey at Vazon Bay and it dropped a lot of *Daily Mirrors*, *Sketches* and *Times* right on to one of Le Riche's lorries. You can't beat that for skill! They were dated August and gave an account of the people taken off Spitzburgen.

I started making a dress for Judith last week, for a twelve-month-old and someone who came in said, 'What is the use? She may be fourteen when she gets it.' Then my heart went down to zero. That was a bit too much for me, so I calmly undid it. I feel very chary about starting one for a fourteen-year-old. I think before the fourteen years are over I shall be pushing up the daisies if I am still a prisoner here. Lots of old people and invalids will die this coming winter, there is not enough to keep them going and nothing to keep them warm in the food line. During the summer holidays the children picked nearly two tons of blackberries and sloes to send to Guernsey for the jam factory. Our sugar was stopped a month ago and we were told by the Germans this was because it meant jam for us this winter, but now after our sacrifice we are calmly told it is going to Germany and France for the troops. We cannot make jam with the mite of sugar we get occasionally.

October 1st, 1941

The weather is beautiful, really hotter than August and bathing still going on. There are no visitors, the boats are fewer and there are many more restrictions but we have only about seven or eight of the German troops here now and lots have left Guernsey. The mark notes we have will be quite worthless after the war, I hate the sight of them. They have collared all our English silver and notes, there is scarcely a silver coin to be seen anywhere. Last Sunday two big shots came over and ordered all the fishermen to meet them at the harbour, then each £10 which they had previously paid was carefully handed back to them in mark notes! As they have collared our good English money it is nothing less than bare-faced robbery. They have a motive for every move they make, systematic robbery is their aim every time. The postman goes down and carries up on his back all the mail we get now, like the good old days of forty years ago when the mail-bags were thrown off the boat at the harbour and the Islanders went down and sorted their own letters.

History is repeating itself all right and it will be tinder boxes and halfpenny dips if we are lucky this winter. I had a nasty fall last week in the bedroom and I tripped over a mat so I have a nice black eye thrown in. My weight has come down to 10 stone 6 pounds from 13 stone.

October 9th, 1941

Today we have all had another proof of German culture. Dubras, the Guernsey hairdresser, has been sending a man over to Sark to do hair-cutting, shampooing and chiropody. This time when visiting Stock's Hotel the German Captain set on him, called him a B— Swiss, hit him in the jaw and almost kicked him out of the Hotel. Not content with that he followed him out all along the lane, shooting from his revolver all the way, calling, 'halt!', and throwing in a number of adjectives. The poor Swiss is trying to make his case good, but the case is not finished yet. The German Captain is the worst hated of all the Germans who have been here. Norah and Elizabeth, from La Valette, had a narrow escape from being shot. Elizabeth had been to see us and Norah was taking her a little way home along the common. They had just got to Stock's Hotel gate when the brute came racing through, firing as he ran. She came in quite scared. I saw part of it through the bedroom window and thought a German had gone mad.

We hear today 150 more German troops are coming to Sark, they mean to fortify Little Sark and are going to erect big guns, etc. The German Commander asked Mrs Hathaway if they could have all the milk and butter they want. She told them we had not got enough for the Sark people now, let alone in the winter. They have bled Guernsey and Jersey white, now they mean to do the same here, swine.

Some jam has come over in tins from France and we are allowed 2oz each. It works out at 2s 6d a pound. We have not had a bit of meat for four weeks until yesterday, then it was ½lb each to last a week, bone, fat and skin included.

Last week we were thrilled by the rumour that an English speed-boat had taken nineteen Germans and an Englishman off Alderney and got safely to England. How pleased we were. Then this week it is absolutely denied. It is amazing the rumours that are put about and the speed at which they travel.

Alas and alack! The German troops have arrived, nearly three hundred, just fancy, nearly as many as the Sark population. Tons of wood, huts and barbed wire have arrived and there are German boats everywhere everyday, delivering the goods, large army lorries, cars and a large delivery van. All feudal laws and customs are broken, and it is hateful to hear cars and motor bikes on our peaceful little Island. The lanes are no longer safe. I have to hold on to the hedge with my eyebrows. (Good job they are strong.)

October 20th, 1941

A mock battle has been staged for today and it is simply hellish. The noise and rattle of the guns from Guernsey are quite deafening, and we are told to keep out of the danger zones or it will be sudden death. Needless to say, we are determined to stay indoors. It goes on from 1pm till 8pm without stopping.

October 21st, 1941

We are still alive, although a large shell dropped on Robert's cottage and they have wired it off from the public and sent for an expert to deal with it. Poor Mrs Rondel's bungalow would have been no more if the shell had exploded. They are laying mines everywhere and putting barbed wire over all the cliffs and bays, so we just have the roads to walk on where the motors make it unsafe. There is a huge swastika over the Bel Air. I hope our RAF sees it, also hoards of unhealthy brutes everywhere. We don't dare be out after dark although the curfew is not until 10pm.

It is amazing how calmly we are all trying to carry on with our work, there is no fear in any of our hearts, only absolute disgust for the whole lot and prayers for their speedy removal.

November 1st, 1941

I have had another birthday and feel twenty years older. It seems strange not hearing from any of you in England and the Red Cross messages are very few these days, owing to lots of boats being sunk in these waters.

There is a big raid on Guernsey and Jersey today, the guns are terrifying at times. We are always afraid of having our house taken for the troops, as nearly every house and room has been taken in Guernsey and all the hotels in Sark, as well as all the unoccupied houses and odd rooms. I don't know where we could go if turned out, for we are not sure of the bungalow even, as all small huts and portable buildings are being seized and the owners not even asked, and if any fuss is made we are told we shall be compensated after the war, I wonder.

Several German soldiers came into church last Sunday and just stood in the aisle never removing their hats (again, German culture). They listened to a prayer or two, then lumbered out, making all the noise they could. The Vicar in his prayer was praying for Russia. While in church at service we heard sixty to eighty going by, singing on a route march, coarse, vulgar brutes. I have been hiding my blankets this week, in case they have a house-to-house search, for it seems I shall never have enough cash any more to replace them. I started making a small cot blanket for Judith, of all odd balls of wool, every colour, quite gay, but we are forced from time to time to unwind a square to darn our clothes and stockings. It is just marvellous how gay we are becoming! Norah has had a pair of wellingtons given her, to pay when we can, so she has handed me her shoes to keep me dry and it is all exchange and barter to keep decently covered.

Miss Hale says it will come to loin cloths to keep decently covered but I sincerely hope not, or it will seem like John Oxenham's novel *Perilous Lovers*. We have had a very cold spell this week and could hardly keep warm.

November 19th, 1941

My Diary does not seem to be written so often, nor does it seem so varied, but the paper shortage is acute. We are quite well. I get depressed and low-spirited some days, it is little wonder, for I never thought we should face another winter like last year. I suppose you all wonder how we are existing and what we are living on. The bank in Guernsey allowed us a small overdraft which will not last many more weeks. How I shall pay it back I don't know.

We had an awful scare this week, we were told 200 more Germans had arrived and we were likely to be turned out of our house. All rooms and houses were to be ready for them. They don't care a hang where people go so long as *they* get comfortable quarters. Well, ours is not wanted yet, but the awful uncertainty is not too good. I went to the Seneschal and implored him to keep off this house. I am quite prepared that they will have the bungalow. There is not a hut, shed or any portable building anywhere in the Island that they have not battered down and taken on the cliffs where they want them for shelter and to hide the infernal guns. They take what furniture they want, the rest they set fire to in the middle of the field and it is quite pathetic to see just the brick chimney-stack standing alone, where once a pretty little home stood. They show no mercy and some of them look villainous. Tons of coal and barrels of paraffin arrive every day for the troops but we get no coal and not even a spot of oil, so there are long dark nights ahead. One cannot even see to knit or read. I am hiding my potatoes for it is our main food and with all these invaders here we shall soon be reduced. They have stored tons and tons of flour for their own use in the hall and art gallery. I think they fear a siege.

December 12th, 1941

Here we are into another Christmas month. We all mean to make the best of it and try to cheer each other up, so we are arranging to carry our food to different houses and share as far as we can. As arrangements stand now, Miss Carter will bring a chicken and Miss MacEwan will bring one also. I will cook them, find the vegetables and entertain these visitors, and in return we will have a nice dinner and grateful I am for it. We have a great deal to be thankful for, I suppose, because we have our own house left us so far. We cannot tell you much in our Red Cross messages, we are not allowed to. 'Walter Wilson' was a huge joke, the greatest part of your message was cut out and we are both wondering what it was you said that did not pass. We each had a message this week.

I am starting to collect some stamps for you. The ones I have missed saving were George V and George VI 2d stamps cut in two to serve as 1d ones until Guernsey started to do the same. £2 and £3 are offered for them already. There is scarcely any British or Guernsey money left, just filthy marks, everywhere, valued here at 2s 2d, in Guernsey at 1s 1d. The States of Guernsey are issuing 6d, 1s, 2s 6d and 5s notes. The Islands will be bankrupt soon if not already so.

We are told the Germans are expecting the British Navy in six weeks. I will be down at the harbour on that day, hugging them around the neck! If these are any samples of Hitler's soldiers they are great cowards, if you could only see how they have barbed wired themselves into their hotels and quarters it would make you laugh, (by the way, the wire they are using here is that which was left by us at Dunkirk). There is practically no firing in France or on the Islands, all is so quiet we wonder what the sudden calm means. Most wirelesses have now given out on the Island. Some people have rigged up what they call the bottle set, 100 small jars, either potted meat jars, or those glass fairy lamps we use at decoration times, and each is filled with sea water. They get the news, but nothing much else, so we go round to different houses asking for news.

As the weeks go by so the stores come to an end. It is really amazing to read the Exchange column and to see the money that is offered for everyday goods. 50s is offered for 1lb of tobacco, the same amount for 1lb of tea, flour, sugar, rice and all things to make puddings with. These are sorely needed, especially by the sick and invalids.

The Germans are offering £3 for half or whole gold sovereigns and of course their worthless mark is offered. I hope everyone sticks to the good old English gold they have.

The Germans are making great preparations for Christmas festivities, they have taken over the hall completely. I believe they are giving tickets to the Islanders, some of whom will accept. They have a funny mentality and one can only put it down to ignorance, but the Germans certainly like the Sark folk better than the English. If they ask you 'Are you Sark?', and you say, 'No, English', they look at you in quite an evil way and you almost think they are going to spit.

Norah has made me a nice, warm, smart dressing-gown for Christmas. I have nothing to give her. We do miss our Christmas letters and gifts from you all, especially the Stockton cake. We are told there is to be beef for Christmas and I have plenty of potatoes and vegetables for all, so all is well for that day, though no champagne like last year. The hotels will be full of German troops. No home or house is the same since they have taken complete command. Thank God, so far, we have none in this house.

December 26th, 1941, Boxing Day

The day is over once again. Our Christmas was most peaceful. We had a nice dinner of chicken, Brussels sprouts, potatoes and all that goes with it and to crown all Miss MacEwan turned up with a grand bottle of claret. She had asked at Stock's Hotel for it and it was very good. We all had two or three glasses each. We could not hear the King's speech, for we are still without the wireless, but Miss Carter and Norah were invited to Miss Robinson's for tea and they heard it there. I had saved a candle to light on Christmas night but Mrs Reb sent me a pint of paraffin on Christmas Eve and it was a godsend. Fancy that we should ever have thought it could give such pleasure.

The little gifts we were able to pass around were really laughable. Some of mine were Brussels sprouts, a candle, a bit of real tea, some aspirins, a bit of salt, a small portion of pepper, one ounce of lemon peel. Mrs Falle gave me one pound of white flour, a handful of currants and a handful of raisins, so with a stroke of luck, I will make a pudding for New Year. On New Year's Day I have promised to cook a duck for friends and we will all dine here, so you see we shall have another free dinner.

The 200 German troops have had their Christmas parties and dances and are leaving today; talk says they are bound for Russia. The same amount of men are arriving in their place who some say are to be Austrians, but we shall know as time goes on. They (the departing ones) had a little service in our church before leaving and the Vicar says they were most reverent. On the whole they have not been too bad, not nearly so noisy or troublesome as the few who were here this time last year.

January 5th, 1942

We had our New Year's feast and it was quite a happy day. I kept a good log fire burning all day long. Thank God we still have plenty of wood to burn and Dr Pittard lets his man come once a week to saw enough to last us all the week, and he pays him to do so. We are surrounded with good kind friends. I have made my pudding and it was quite good, not rich, but if we ever have rich food again we must have some liver pills ready, it is sure to upset us. Norah wants chocolate and sugar and plum cake, and lots of it. We each had a little packet of sweets for Christmas from the shop, about an ounce, and went nearly crazy about them. The new German troops have arrived and such an awful lot they are, quite young and raw. They fired guns the whole of New Year's Eve and during the day, just frantically, anywhere and everywhere. Then on New Year's night there was a big attack on Guernsey by our RAF, even Little Sark was lit up by the fires. I believe they are afraid of a landing like in Norway. None of them have topcoats and they look cold, their uniforms are even more threadbare than the last ones, and some of them have big patches on their knees and behinds of just ordinary sailcloth, like tents are made of. They ask at the cottages if they can come in and get warm. Mrs Sharp at Little Sark has twenty-seven of them billeted on her, and she says some of them have no shirts and if they stoop to do anything the pullover runs up and shows their naked skin and you know what a bleak coast it is at Port Gorey and the Coupée, where they keep watch.

Grand Dixcart, home of the author Mrs Julia Tremayne and her daughter Norah during the Occupation.

1st July, 1940.

To the Chief of the Military and Civil Authorities
Jersey (St. Helier).

1. I intend to neutralize military establishments in Jersey by occupation.

2. As evidence that the Island will surrender the military and other establishments without resistance and without destroying them, a large White Cross is to be shown as follows, from 7 a.m. July 2nd. 1940.

   a. In the centre of the Airport in the East of the Island.
   b. On the highest point of the fortifications of the port.
   c. On the square to the North of the Inner Basin of the Harbour.

   Moreover all fortifications, buildings, establishments and houses are to show the White Flag.

3. If these signs of peaceful surrender are not observed by 7 a.m. July 2nd, heavy bombardment will take place.

   a. Against all military objects.
   b. Against all establishments and objects useful for defence.

4. The signs of surrender must remain up to the time of the occupation of the Island by German troops.

5. Representatives of the Authorities must stay at the Airport until the occupation.

6. All Radio traffic and other communications with Authorities outside the Island will be considered hostile actions and will be followed by bombardment.

7. Every hostile action against my representatives will be followed by bombardment.

8. In case of peaceful surrender, the lives, property, and liberty of peaceful inhabitants are solemnly guaranteed.

The Commander of the German Air Forces in Normandie,
General

The States have ordered this Communication to be printed and posted forthwith, and charge the Inhabitants to keep calm, to comply with the requirements of the Communication and to offer no resistance whatsoever to the occupation of the Island.

The communication from the Commander of the German Air Forces in Normandy, addressed to the Governor of Jersey on July 1st, 1940, and announcing the Occupation of the Island by German troops.

Above: La Seigneurie, official residence of the Seigneurs of Sark. In the foreground are the only doves allowed on the Island.

Below: The signature of the German Commandant, Dr Lanz, written first in German script and then in Latin characters, as it appears in the visitors' book at La Seigneurie.

The Commandant Dr
Lanz (centre), with
Lieutenant Muller (left)
and Dr Maas, German
officers serving on the
Island.

The Avenue, Sark's
'main street', in peace-
time.

Guernsey, 1940—the evacuation of women and children.

Percy Brown, Sark's postman, delivering mail on August Bank Holiday, one month after the German Occupation.

A group of German officers on Harbour Hill.

A German motor vehicle crossing La Coupée, the narrow neck of land which connects Sark with Little Sark.

These German soldiers, photographed at the harbour, look happy enough, but by the end of the Occupation most were weak with hunger and reduced to begging or stealing from the Islanders to supplement their meagre rations.

News from England

TO THE CHANNEL-ISLANDERS

All of you, His Majesty's loyal subjects on the Channel Islands, must keep asking yourselves two great questions :—" How long must we put up with the German occupation ? " and " How are our friends on the mainland ? "

This news-sheet brings you the heartening answers. We on the mainland are in good heart. By subjecting our women and children to the wickedest form of warfare known to history, Hitler has only stiffened our backs. And the events of the last three weeks have only served to confirm Mr. Churchill's words of August 21st, that " the road to victory may not be so long as we expect." Nor may the day be so distant when we shall come to your relief. All our rapidly and enormously increasing strength is directed towards that day when the shadow of the bully will be lifted from you and from the whole of Europe. We shall continue to bring you the news from England as often and as regularly as we can.

A MESSAGE FROM HIS MAJESTY THE KING

The Queen and I desire to convey to you our heartfelt sympathy in the trials which you are now enduring. We earnestly pray for your speedy liberation, knowing that it will surely come.

GEORGE R. I.

Bombs over Germany

Hitler has suffered his first major defeat. While the mass raids on Britain have been broken up at a devastating cost to the Luftwaffe, the Royal Air Force carries out nightly raids on Germany and the Occupied Territories with such precision and intensity that the Hitler war machine has been visibly weakened.

The attacks on Germany have now lasted three months. From the North Sea to the borders of Czechoslovakia, from the Baltic to the Swiss Frontier, there is no military objective which is safe from them. Across the Alps, too, heavy blows have been struck at such targets in Milan, Turin, Genoa and other industrial centres.

Only military targets are attacked, but the effect has been that much the more serious. It contrasts

Thuringia outside Berlin, walls of flame have closed even in hidden factories and munition stores until explosions broke out.

Besides these blows at the heart of Germany, the fortified ports in Norway, Holland, Belgium and France, where the Germans are concentrating for the suicidal attempt at invasion, have been repeatedly struck.

In Africa and Italian possessions in the Mediterranean a similar story has been written by the R.A.F. with the difference that the Italian anti-aircraft defences and fighting planes are weaker than the German.

UP AND UP

groups of employees, towns and suburbs have presented Spitfires and Hurricanes to the nation. Every kind of group has subscribed, some it has even come from people bearing the same christian name—the Harolds, the Georges, etc.

From everywhere come fighters and bombers, and fighters, most of all Squadrons of Spitfires.

Morale-boosting newspapers and pamphlets such as these were dropped over the Islands by the RAF

News from England

GERMAN FRONT LINE BATTERED

Dover, September 28.

WATCHERS on this coastline will never forget the skies of moving light and fire which they have seen night after night in recent weeks enveloping, like an Aurora Borealis of the south, the ports where the Germans are massed for their attempted invasion.

With merciless regularity the R.A.F. have destroyed the enemy barges, their stores, barracks, fuel and ammunition dumps.

Over Boulogne on the 18th the raids appeared to start as soon as " p.m. with greater violence than usual, and as they developed, many miles of the French coastline seemed to be ablaze. Thus fresh waves of bombers spread the attack to Calais, where great fires broke out and lit the sky with a feverish glow which spread.

On the 24th our bombers raided Calais for 7 hours.

The raids have effected the entire span of the German outposts.

Cherbourg

Cherbourg had special attention on the 17th. The Air Ministry states that this particular port caused " industrious havoc to ships and docks."

[remaining text illegible]

General Effect

[illegible]

Mediterranean

[illegible]

American View

"Sticking the Neck Out"

"YOU'RE TELLING ME!"

Latest in the Gallup survey of U.S. public opinion was the question. Recently the Germans claimed they had shot down 427 English planes in one week, and lost only 99 of their own. Do you think this was accurate? " Voting was: No, 86%; Yes, 3%; Don't know 11%.

The eighth poll in successive question in America of late shows that 42% are back Britain compared with 37% in July.

BOMBS FOR BERLIN

The systematic destruction of Germany's war industry by the R.A.F. has continued steadily in the second half of September.

STRANGLEHOLD BY THE NAVY

SEA POWER, decisive factor in all great wars, remains firmly in the hands of Britain. September has brought more proofs of this.

More and More

[illegible]

LEAVES AND NEWS

AUTUMN leaves are falling, as well as your copies of News from England. They may seem a gloomy enough reminder that the summer is over and a second war winter is setting in, this one under the alien heel of German hurt on world dominion.

But remember that the leaves must seem far more ominous to the Germans. They remind them of the Kaiser's promise to his armies in 1914 : " You will be back before the leaves fall" and of Hitler's repeated earlier promise which was to celebrate the occupation of London in August.

[illegible]

Cheer up!!

ESCAPE FROM GUERNSEY

Eight Reach Britain

London, September 27

A PARTY of eight men have successfully escaped from Guernsey to England in a 20 ft. boat. The London press is headlining their adventures.

They left Guernsey under cover of darkness and rowed half a mile before using the motor. When they were about two miles out four flares were dropped by three German planes flying over them. One fell only twenty yards from the boat, but they were not seen.

Just after passing the Caskets their engine broke down, but the repairs were finished in four hours and they eventually sighted Start Point, the landmark for which they were making.

The party consisted of Mr. Frederick Hockey, 47, a signalman employed by the harbour administration at St. Peter port, three of his sons, Frederick, 25, George, 21, and Harold 16, who were engaged in tomato growing, and Messrs. William Mahy, Percy de Port, William Dorey and Herbert Bichard, independent growers.

All beaches were mined.

German soldiers
excavating the remains
of a bomb found in the
garden next to the
Vicarage.

During the early days of the Occupation,
German troops found Sark public houses well
stocked with beer and spirits. Soldiers always
removed their belts and sidearms when on
licensed premises.

Two soldiers who were killed when clearing
their own mines immediately after the
Occupation are buried in the cemetery near St
Peter's Church.

German preparations for blowing up the harbour at St Peter Port, Guernsey.

In spite of the German order to hand in all receivers (*left*), a few well concealed sets kept the Islanders in touch with the outside world (*Evening News*, May 15th, 1945).

BEKANNTMACHUNG

Spionagefälle auf der Insel Guernsey machen weitere Massnahmen erforderlich.

Auf Grund eines Befehls des Bez. Chef A werden sämtliche Rundfunk Empfangsgerate der Zivilbevölkerung bis auf weiteres beschlagnahmt und in Verwahrung genommen. Die Gerate sind bis zum 20.11.40 abzugeben. Ort und Stunde für die Angabe werden vom Controlling Committee of the States of Guernsey bekanntgegeben werden. Auf jeden Gerat ist vom Ablieferer ein Zettel zu kleben, auf dem Name und Anschrift des Eigentümers ersichtlich ist.

Für den Fall der Nichtablieferung werden hiermit auf Grund der Verordnung vom 10.9.40 in Verbindung mit § 1 der Verordnung vom 23.8.40 (Verordnungsblatt, Mil. Verw. Frankreich Seite 72 und 86) Ordnungsstrafen und zwar Haft bis zu 6 Wochen und Geldstrafen bis zu RM. 30.000.— angedroht.

Der Feldkommandant.
gez. Schumacher.
Oberst.

Den 11. November 1940.

NOTICE

The favouring of espionage in the Island of Guernsey makes further measures necessary.

By virtue of an Order from District Chief A, all Wireless Receiving Sets of the Civil population will be requisitioned until further notice and deposited into a place of safety. The sets are to be delivered by Midnight on November 20, 1940. Place and time of delivery will be indicated by the Controlling Committee of the States of Guernsey. A label bearing the name and address of the owner is to be pasted on each set by the deliverer.

In case of non-delivery, in virtue of the Order of the 10.9.40, in conection with Para. 1 of Order dated 23.8.40. (Order Sheet, Military Administration in France pages 72 and 86) penalties amounting to not more than 6 weeks imprisonment and fines up to RM. 30,000 may be imposed.

The Feldkommandant
signed : Schumacher
Colonel.

11th November, 1940.

Order Respecting Wireless Receiving Sets.

By the direction of the German Feldkommandant THE CONTROLLING COMMITTEE OF THE STATES OF GUERNSEY (hereinafter called "the Committee") makes the following ORDER —

Every person in this Island in possession of a Wireless Receiving Set of any description must deliver such Set or cause it to be delivered to one of the Official Collectors appointed for the purpose. All Batteries must be removed from the Sets before delivery. (SEE SARK NOTICE)

The Committee in order to assist the inhabitants will arrange for collecting Sets and it is intended that such will take possession Friday the 15th instant at 8.45 a.m.

Persons awaiting the collection of their Sets and whose premises may be left unattended should arrange with neighbours to give delivery of their Sets when the Official Collector calls. However half hour than once.

Every Set must bear the name and postal address of the person giving up possession written plainly on a label ADHERING to the outside of the Set. Tie-on labels may be added but are not compulsory. Adhesive labels are obligatory.

An identification number will be given for every Set delivered to serve as a receipt and such receipt must be carefully preserved.

If a Set is not collected by an Official Collector before November 19th the person in possession of the Set must immediately communicate with the Constables of his Parish for further directions.

Anyone in default will be liable to a fine not exceeding 30,000 Reichmarks or to imprisonment up to six weeks or to both of such penalties.

GUERNSEY, this Thirteenth day of November, 1940.

JOHN LEALE.
For and on behalf of the Controlling
Committee of the States of Guernsey.

Genehmigt (Approved)
Nebenstelle Guernsey
der Feldkommandantur 515
DR. REFFLER.
Kriegsverwaltungsrat.
den 13.11.40.

TWO MEN RAN
GUERNSEY RADIO

HELPER DIED IN HORROR CAMP

WHEN 48-year-old Ludovic Edmund Bertrand, of Longstone Vinery, and Reg. Warley (38), both of St. Peter Port, learned that Germans had confiscated all wireless sets, Bertrand decided that the people of Guernsey should have the news.

He got a one-valve radio set of battery type; his aerial was the product of a sabotage raid on the German telephone system, he got a battery by night from a German lorry, returned it each morning and operated his receiving station between the German electricity station and the ack-ack headquarters.

'Victory in the West' starring Adolf Hitler,
showing at the Gaumont Palace, Guernsey.
This notice appeared inside the cinema.

NOTICE

FOR German films with English sub-titles the left-hand section of the stalls are reserved for <u>Civilians only</u>; the right-hand section and the Balcony for German troops only.

Hubert Lanyon (left) in his bakery in Sark. He was jailed for distributing copies of the *Guernsey Underground News Service* (GUNS).

Soldiers relaxing outside the Bel Air Hotel (German Headquarters until it was accidentally destroyed by fire).

Above: Visitors to Sark during 1940 were few and far between and most wore field grey uniforms. A swastika is painted at the tunnel entrance to the Island, next to the harbour.

Opposite: Since all other means of communication with the mainland were denied to the Islanders, the Red Cross 'postal service' provided an invaluable link with family and friends.

Below: One of the four 30.5cm emplacements for Battery Mirus in Guernsey.

From:

WAR ORGANISATION OF THE BRITISH RED CROSS
AND ORDER OF ST. JOHN

To:
Comité International
de la Croix Rouge
Genève

Prisoners of War,
Wounded and Missing
Department

ENQUIRER
Fragesteller

Name .... HAMON

Christian name .... Mrs VIOLET
Vorname

Address .... RED CROSS MESSAGE BUREAU,

No 751.

GADDUM HOUSE, 16, QUEEN ST.,

MANCHESTER, 2, ENGLAND.

Relationship of Enquirer to Addressee ...... SISTER
Wie ist Fragesteller mit Empfänger verwandt?

The Enquirer desires news of the Addressee and asks that the following
message should be transmitted to him.
Der Fragesteller verlangt Auskunft über den Empfänger. — Bitte um Weiter-
beförderung dieser Meldung.

DEAR TOM PHIL ALL WELL HOPE
YOU ARE THE SAME. MUM
DAD ELSIE. MY LOVE
DOROTHY'S CHILDREN O.K.
VIOLET

Date .... 24 May 1941

ADDRESSEE
Empfänger

Name .... LANGLOIS

Christian name .... THOMAS
Vorname

Address .... 18 CORNET ST.

ST PETER PORT

GUERNSEY C.I

The Addressee's reply to be written overleaf.

THESE 60,000 BRITONS?

diphtheria and whooping cough have broken out. Soon there will be a renewal of the virulent flu that took a heavy toll of the islands in the winter of 1940.

In the hospitals they have no anæsthetics any more. The surgeons will not undertake operations unless it is a matter of life and death, and then the patient must suffer the lancet's probe in stoic silence.

In the General Hospital at St. Helier, where the Germans occupy the two main floors, even the sterilisation of instruments for use on civilian patients is now forbidden. It uses up fuel.

Long ago they tore up the last of the sheets to make bandages.

The doctors cannot heal. They have no drugs of any kind left.

It is only in extreme cases that patients are allowed extra food. Even then it is only a handful of rice.

£20 Frocks

There is practically nothing to buy in the shops. There are no shoes—and here again the children suffer most. A few shirts—rationed—at £2. For the women a few shoddy frocks at £15 to £20. For the men very occasionally can be found a reach-me-down suit at £25. And naturally the people haven't got all that money.

★

FOOD stocks dwindling to pinpoint, medical supplies non-existent. That is the picture on the Channel Islands today. Even in these terrible conditions there might be a fighting chance for these Britons if they had the will to survive. But their will has been sapped. They have practically lost hope.

"All these years," said one of them to me, "We have listened secretly at the radio for the news from London running the

ENGLISH CHANNEL

BOURNEMOUTH
WEYMOUTH
CHERBOURG
ALDERNEY
GUERNSEY
SARK
JERSEY
MILES
10 20 30 40 50

Nazi sailor, Island "Bobby"—One of the few pictures smuggled out.

NAZIS AND BRITISH HAVE TO LIVE SIDE BY SIDE ONLY 75 MILES FROM BRITAIN

peet that faces the Channel Islanders.

What can we do about it, for we are certainly not indifferent to their fate?

First thought, of course, is that we should evacuate them by sending a few ships over, for after all civilians were evacu-

any hope to the starving islanders.

1—ATTACK THE ISLANDS AT ONCE AND RESCUE OUR FELLOW-BRITONS.

It could undoubtedly be done, but it might cost thousands of soldiers' lives. The islands are guarded by miles of dangerous, rock-strewn sea, with intricate channels. And, in addition, mostly by formidable cliffs. There can be no doubt the Germans have heavily fortified the few tiny beaches available for landing.

Paratroops dropped on Jersey's one small airfield could be mown down in scores as they landed.

And—we all know the technique of invasion by now—it would have to be preceded by

take time and some delicate negotiations.

We couldn't just send ships over, shouting, "Oi, don't shoot. We're bringing food." The Germans would naturally suspect a trick and sink the ships at sight.

No, this is how it would have to be fixed.

The British Government approaches the British Red Cross who get in touch with the International Red Cross at Geneva. They in turn inform the German Red Cross in Berlin, who communicate with the German Government.

Long Job

The answer must come back by the same circuitous route and then lengthy negotiations about details would do the same.

It might easily take months. And then the German High Command, who would have th...

Above and opposite: How the British press saw the Occupation of the Channel Islands.

Huns whip slaves to death on British soil

THE Germans are using foreigners as slaves, whipping them to death, on British territory—Guernsey, in the Channel Isles—the House of Commons was told yesterday.

Major Vyvyan Adams (Con., Leeds W.) read this extract from a report by a Briton who has escaped from the island:

"Their general condition is too terrible for words. They were landed in a practically starving condition, their only clothing being cement bags.

"It is nothing unusual for them to be whipped at their work until they drop dead. They are then picked up by the arms and legs and flung into a lorry.

"There was no burial—the bodies remained there until loads of rubbish from the quarries were tipped on top of them. What the sanitary conditions are going to be like I dare not think."

"We have a score to settle with the Germans," Major Adams added, "as well as the subject peoples of Europe, and we may be sure the Germans will fight desperately to avoid their own defeat.

"They won't believe that defeat is going to mean anything for them but their extermination."

CHANNEL ISLES RECORD

References to music, theatricals, tennis, cricket, bathing and dancing appear in cheerful messages from the Channel Islands which have recently reached the Red Cross in London.

The record number of 7,000 messages have been received from the islands during the past three weeks.

Above left: Daily Mirror, February 23rd, 1944; *above right: Daily Telegraph*, January 1st, 1944.

Right: Rationing: with gas and electricity severely rationed, lamps like this were made, using a piece of string as a wick and a little diesel oil or paraffin as fuel.

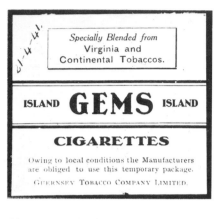

Specially Blended from
Virginia and
Continental Tobaccos.

ISLAND **GEMS** ISLAND

CIGARETTES

Owing to local conditions the Manufacturers are obliged to use this temporary package.
GUERNSEY TOBACCO COMPANY LIMITED.

Cigarettes and tobacco were also in extremely short supply. Each Island had its own system of tobacco rationing.

STATES OF GUERNSEY

TOBACCO AND TOBACCO PRODUCTS.

EACH COUPON entitles the Holder to purchase One Ration of Tobacco and Tobacco Products on or after the date prescribed on the Coupon.

30	29	28	27	26
May 26th 1941	May 19th 1941	May 12th 1941	May 5th 1941	Apr. 28th 1941

January 11th, 1942

It is bitterly cold, our first snow and we feel we want more to eat. They are bringing us less food from France. I suppose now there are no more goods to give in exchange from Guernsey so they will keep us short. I hope the bread does not give out. What would I not give for a home-made Stockton loaf with plenty of butter on!

For a week now there have been continuous raids on Brest, very heavy indeed, and all the troops here and in Guernsey are most uneasy for they are afraid of parachutists landing, so they lie hidden in the hedges and all cubby-holes ready to fire on anyone who looks suspicious. I tell you it is not safe to be out, especially after dark. If dogs are found they are shot on sight. It is very difficult to feed the animals, they are sick of potatoes and our potatoes may not last long anyway. If, God forbid, we should be here another winter it is the carpets and the furniture we shall be eating! Clothes, too, are a serious problem. I am making some house slippers out of rug wool and soling them with bits of old mackintosh. Norah lends me her shoes so we cannot go out at the same time.

January 17th, 1942

A very heavy raid on Guernsey harbour and lots of shipping bombed. We never hear of the death toll and the cause of death is never in print. There were some poor Poles working for the Germans on the White Rock and a great many of them were killed. How those poor Poles are being persecuted. Previous to coming to Guernsey they were in Alderney working. The ships that were bombed were loaded with cement and guns for France.

Since writing last Mr Baird has been taken away to a prison camp, we don't know exactly what for. He was an American, but used to report at German Headquarters every week, so it cannot be for that. It appears he said in one of his Red Cross messages that there were 200 or 300 troops in Sark, so we think that must be the reason. He has asked the Vicar to take charge of his house as he never expects to get home again. It is all very sad.

Last week the Germans broke into Mr Bradbury's house and studio. They stripped the house of all furniture, smashed up a lot of it to make fires and broke up the whole of the wooden studio for firewood. It is pathetic to see the splintered glass and picture mounts lying about. I don't know what they have done with his nice pictures. Another example of German culture. Mrs Rondel's house is used as a wireless station; there are heavy guns in her back garden and deep trenches in her flower garden and she has two or three rooms only to herself. It is not safe for her to be there because if the RAF drops a bomb on the lighthouse it will wipe that whole part out.

January 26th, 1942

The Bel Air Hotel is on fire and almost gutted out (Headquarters of the Germans). Never has there been such a fire on Sark, and of course, no water or appliances to put it out. When some barrels of petrol caught fire we thought the whole of Sark was done for, the explosion was terrific. What furniture was saved has been broken up for firewood for the Germans, lovely polished tables and chairs, blankets, linen and silver all gone. The Germans seem to have a mania for breaking up things, especially glass, there is broken glass everywhere. If they go into an unoccupied house and there are any lovely bookcases, they burn the books and smash every pane of glass and some of the bookcases are antiques which can never be replaced. The Sark Art Gallery is now used for a munitions store.

The grazing fields are being taken for gun emplacements, and in Guernsey too, and some of the farmers have to get rid of their cattle, so that means less milk and less butter.

They have been having raids in Guernsey and Alderney for several nights and many ships have been sunk by our RAF in the harbour. The Sark divers have been sent for to go to Guernsey and get some of the wreckage up, including a great number of poor Frenchmen who were forced to come and work here. A Frenchman told Walter Hamon they (about forty or fifty) were coming out of the cinema in France one evening when they were arrested, marched off to a boat and shipped for Guernsey, and now poor fellows they are at the bottom of the sea. There were a great number of horses also on the White Rock, either being landed or being shipped away, and they were blown to bits.

February 1st, 1942

A Red Cross message from you today. I am so pleased little Judith is doing so well. By now Collins will be called up and I hope you will keep cheery and get someone to live with you for company. We keep well in spite of the shortages and the weather is improving. We have a bowl of early primroses on the table, so it tells of spring. I begin to feel like a 'wandering minstrel', a 'thing of shreds and patches'. We darn and patch and unpick and reknit all day long, but it is our poor feet that won't keep warm. I suppose it is the lack of good food. I have chilblains for the first time in my life.

We have all come to the conclusion that Sark is in a very sticky position, the guns from Guernsey and Jersey can reach us so when they are firing at our planes the shrapnel bursts all over the Island.

Thirty tons of coal went up in smoke when the Bel Air Hotel was on fire. The Germans had it stored for their own use. Only the shell now remains of a once lovely building of Jersey granite, just a skeleton. When the fire started and was burning fiercely all the carts and horses were ordered out by the Germans to try and rescue some of the things. Florida and her husband told me they had to go almost into the fire, they were made to do so by the Germans, although she was terrified. Some of the Sark people had never seen a fire in their lives. Such a blaze, no attempt could be made to save it, so it burned itself out in the early hours of the morning. Granny Guille is being buried today, she was ninety-four or ninety-five, the oldest inhabitant. Madame Durand is ninety-two and still hale and hearty. In Guernsey the death toll is enormous, due mostly to worry and lack of food, not just old people either. I noticed in the Exchange column of the Press someone offers her wedding dress, veil and halo for potatoes! Poor old Mary, or Margot (our old cook), came to me yesterday for some old crusts or stale bread, scraps of any kind, or wood to keep them warm, so you see the state of affairs here. We could give her wood, but nothing else. Poor old soul.

February 11th, 1942

We hear today the three battleships have gone down along the Channel in the night in a fog from Brest, and we are greatly surprised for we thought they were quite done for after the terrible bangings and explosions we have heard for months. Norah saw them and came in and said, 'I have seen three enormous ships go by', the fatal three, we little thought which they were at the time. Also we hear with deep regret the loss of Singapore. It is bitterly cold here and we are having heavy frosts.

I wonder how long I can keep up this Diary. We cannot get any paper or envelopes. I shall be sorry to have to stop because someone may like to glance over it some day. Yesterday was Shrove Tuesday. I could not make the famous pancake; no eggs, no flour, hard luck! Mrs Rondel has six or eight Germans billeted on her and they are tearing her beautiful books in half and feeding the anthracite stove.

No one will ever find these books intact again. We have been most thankful to lend and exchange books, it has been our salvation, but soon I suppose they will be exhausted.

March 1st, 1942

Never in my whole life did I think we should be so reduced for everything we need. The shortages are getting worse daily and sometimes we go hungry to bed.

It is all roots that we seem to exist on, parsnips, turnips, carrots and a few potatoes, but these are getting very short indeed. The poor people of Guernsey are begging the potato peelings from those who are lucky enough to have them, and boiling them to eat. They are making parsnip cakes and limpet cakes. Even the vegetables are only for the rich. Turnips are 1s each, or are even sold in slices. People are standing in rows waiting their turn and if all is sold out some go away empty-handed. It is pathetic to hear about it.

It has been the coldest winter in the Channel Isles for ninety-nine years and we could have well done without it. Sawdust is being sold in Guernsey for fire fuel. There is no coal to be had and very few logs—there has been a big demand on the few trees there. Fires may only be lit at about 7 or 8pm so that the people may get warm before going to bed. All this on top of the empty tummy has told many a tale! The crime wave is awful there, shops of all sorts are being broken into. They break the glass in bread shops and with long spikes get the loaves out that way.

Mock battles take place frequently in both Islands and the noise of the guns and the mad behaviour of the troops is amazing. They burst into anyone's garden, over flower beds and vegetables, fully equiped for battle, shooting madly everywhere, and they even walk into the houses. They come right into the living-room and stand looking vacant as they cannot speak English and we cannot speak German. If they don't come in they come and stare into the windows with their ugly faces pressed to the glass. There is an order out this week that all dogs are to be shot at sight if found off the lead. The reason is that several dogs have bitten some of the Germans—it shows their good sense, doesn't it? Another order out this week is that we have to grow and provide for the troops. A bit more of the heel coming down. There is a potato famine everywhere and seed is very scarce. Luckily we saved some so we will try to plant them and hope the Germans won't pinch them when they are ready. There are about 200 of them to feed now.

March 22nd, 1942

Nothing much seems to happen these days or is it that I am getting careless and lazy? Some days I lose heart, and am very dismal. I wonder if I shall ever get off the Island again, or if I shall ever see Judith. Everyone seems to have tummy troubles, and worst of all, we have very few remedies. Drugs are very scarce and hard to get and they mostly come from Germany, so the whole population could easily be wiped off the map if they get to hate us more.

There is a big shortage of doctors. In Guernsey there are only about six or seven doctors for thousands of people and if an epidemic were to break out it would be very serious. They nearly all left the Islands, including our MO.

There were forty-three large barges in Guernsey Harbour last week taking food away. When the flour, tomato and grape industries were stopped, the Guernsey growers planted the greenhouses with early vegetables and potatoes, and as the troops have none I suppose they will have the lot. When the Guernsey men refused to work for the Germans, Poles, French, Luxemburgers and many more were sent to take their place. I have not been to Guernsey since the Occupation, but I believe it is indescribable for filth and dirt. Their quarters are in Cornet Street and the poor fellows have no boots or clothes and lots have been killed or drowned by our RAF when they raided the harbour. These men are forced to work wherever they are wanted.

March 29th, 1942, Palm Sunday

A lovely Sunday morning and so peaceful. These last three nights it has been brilliant moonlight and the noise of guns and bombs has been terrific, and there have been planes over this house all night long. It is no use getting up or being afraid but it is ghastly to think of what does go over our heads while we sleep, or try to sleep. We know they are our planes and that does help to give us courage. We don't know what does really happen and everyone has a different rumour in the mornings to tell. Most of it seems to be bombing troop ships and convoys between here and France, also ships in Guernsey Harbour.

All horses and carts were ordered to be at the top of Goulet one morning to take lots of guns and munitions to the harbour, so that seems a good sign.

The garden looks lovely, full of daffodils and all sorts of flowers. Hitler cannot blight the spring flowers, or check the song of the birds or the wild noises of the seagulls following the plough. Everyone is busy digging and planting all they can get, making more preparations for next winter than they made for this, although each one of us feels we shall be free by then. It is only that feeling that carries us on and the confident hopes we have of victory. Someone who has been to Guernsey for a few days tells us of all the misery and hardships of the poor Guernsey folk. He saw people clamouring for potato *peelings* at 3d a lb and saw some coming away in tears because all was sold out before their turn came.

April 5th, 1942, Easter Sunday

A beautiful sunny morning. We hear that a gang of seventy or a hundred more men are coming to Sark to make roads and tunnels, and one road is to cut right through Stock's Hotel and join the Little Sark road. So, if needs be, they will cut through our garden, who knows? Perhaps the houses will be demolished, they have been pulled down in Guernsey for the same purpose. A cement road is to be made to Port Carey and Mrs Walbroath was turned back one day, off her own property, and told she no longer owned any property in Sark, it was all German, and forever!

Guns are fixed everywhere, even in the Vicarage garden and pointing towards the church. We wonder if a shower of bullets will greet us some day when coming out, and although anything might happen any day, it is surprising how calmly we carry on. I think that amazes the Germans, for they get quite het up when our planes go over, then all the guns begin to roar over all the Islands and tin hats and barricades are well to the fore.

At one house in Guernsey where the Germans were refused eggs, they found all their hens gone the next day, their heads were cut off and left on the floor. They all seem so cruel in their destruction. George Toplis's bungalow has been broken into this week and everything they had no use for was smashed and trampled on.

April 16th, 1942

All our telephones are out of order and the cables are broken so we stand entirely alone. No one knows when a boat will come or what it will bring. All information is to be had from the German Commandant, the two postmen just wait at the top of the harbour hill before going down for any likely mail until they are told that a boat has arrived.

A lot of German artists arrived last week to give a show in the hall, such an awful lot, it quite gave me a turn to see them. Some of the Sarkees were invited and they went. The lot billeted at Stock's Hotel went clean mad one night and smashed up nearly all the furniture in the hall and dining-room and began shooting at bottles in the fire-place and broke all the nice tiles. They are bad enough without drink but if drunk they go clean mad. Most of the people where they are billeted say they are badly fed, so if that is so, they drown their sorrows in drink. It is very amusing to pass their Headquarters when their midday meal is given out. They all stand outside the window and the meat and vegetables are handed out. They all have slop-pails (white enamel) to carry the soup away in and it looks like good thick dish-water with a few floating vegetables. Norah calls it 'slop-pail parade'!

Someone offers £4 for 1lb of tea this week, and £7 for a golden sovereign, (that is a German wanting the latter).

There are great preparations for Hitler's birthday here and at the Headquarters. A new flagstaff and swastika well in evidence. I gazed into the stock-room when passing the old Vicarage (HQ since they burnt the Bel Air Hotel). There are carcasses of all kinds, chickens, sausages and so on. The officers seem to feed all right but the troops continue to go from farm to farm asking for milk, butter etc. One who has just returned from leave in Germany, says out of twenty-four hours' leave he spent seventeen in an air raid shelter and he brought his kiddies' boots back to Guernsey to be repaired, and he also says there is a shortage of food there. In our *Guernsey Press* this week the Germans say 'England is on the verge of starvation'. I wonder. If you could read it and see all the lies it would open your eyes. I am keeping them all, for some day you might be interested. Hitler says the Channel Island newspapers are eagerly read by all the German people and they are all learning English there, and he hopes the Islanders here will learn German and so help the troops and one another. How nice! I wonder if Hitler knows that Victor Hugo said 'The Channel Islands were bits of France picked up by England'. Is it likely England is going to make them a present to Germany? Some of the Island folk say and think they will be given back to France, but I hope not, for I love my England. We heard the broadcast about us not being forgotten in the Channel Isles, and it was very comforting. We know it is impossible to send us food, the Germans would take it from us. They take all we should have *now*. Last week they took 100 tons of potatoes from Guernsey, new ones, for the troops. The poor Guernsey folk after planting and growing them only got 1lb per head a week for themselves, while here in Sark we have to grow for the Guernsey people and the Germans. Someone said last week that Boston USA was sending food by Red Cross to the Islands. I wish it were true, America has a great love for these little Islands, lots visited Sark and loved it in peace-time.

April 24th, 1942

At Le Chalet (Mrs Judkin's House) this week they have had huge bonfires in the garden of all surplus furniture that happens to be in their way in the house. Settees, armchairs, a bath chair and all sorts of good things. I saw and brought away yesterday two nice solid brass stools to put the kettle on, in perfect condition. They had been thrown into the flames. I rescued them and may be able to have them cleaned one day. Mrs Bateman's lovely house has been practically stripped. The doors and locks broken and the windows smashed, everywhere in disorder.

April 28th, 1942

Today a terrible thing has happened. The German doctor has been found dead in bed. Some rumour says it is suicide, some say it is murder, so you see how serious it is for the Island. All boats are forbidden to leave the Island or any to land here and the houses have all been searched to find likely clues. Nine or ten men, special German police and two officers took part, set out at 4am and entered houses while people were still in bed. Fortunately we were up when they came but everything was topsy-turvy and no beds were made. Beds were turned over and cupboards and drawers were well overhauled. I am certain it is no Sark person if there has been any foul play. The doctor was well liked and a good sportsman and did not appear to have an enemy anywhere.

May 2nd, 1942

Detectives and the Gestapo are still here and they are very active. Suspicion seems to hang on everybody and we go about like the 'Jackdaw of Rheims'. No one is allowed to leave the Island still. We have no dentist here or doctor practising. If we are mad with toothache or ill, heaven help us. Thank goodness the weather is warm and beautiful.

May 9th, 1942

Now the German doctor's batman is missing and it is proved to be murder of Dr Goebels, not suicide. The batman was a Czech. There was a rumour last week we were all to be evacuated to France and that we could only take hand luggage and enough rations for two or three days. The thought of it makes me go cold.

May 20th, 1942

Search is still going on for the missing batman. The Germans have taken away the doctor's body for burying. His head was terribly battered in, it was a most brutal murder. The Sark men have to report every day at HQ and if they are late or don't turn up there are more punishments. Islanders of seventy or eighty-five have to report as well and some of them are too ill to go out.

The batman's body has been found in a well at Vieux Clos, which is seventy or eighty feet deep, but he is said to have left a letter to say he was innocent, so it makes it still harder for the residents. We are all watched and all the young girls especially. When they got the body up it was put in a plain deal box and buried in a field on the Eperquerie. He said he did not do it but was driven to commit suicide because he was so worried and was watched and made prisoner in the dead man's room with an armed guard outside the door. He said the Gestapo drove him mad with questions. We are daily expecting another search of our houses, they are looking for a mallet or a certain kind of stick that was used, a gold watch and a missing wallet or any other clue. Norah says, 'Mother, will you burn that diary you are writing before they search again', but mother says, 'No, not on your life after all my trouble, it may bring me a few shillings after the war, to help pay my debts.' So I have found a safe cubby-hole where even she cannot find it, and as shooting seems to be the penalty for most things I must make my cubby-hole very safe. For we all know it is not only the guilty who suffer, but the friends and relations who are left behind.

June 1st, 1942

A most heavenly summer day. Now it is hot enough for bathing and we all miss the lovely bays, but no one is allowed to go to them, they are so heavily mined. Grande Grève is the only one not mined as that one is well covered with guns on the Coupée, so the German troops go there and bathe naked, in fact they go about the Island more or less nude and sunbathe everywhere, they are a dirty, disgusting lot.

The black cat has brought us in two small rabbits, we had them for dinner. Our money (the bank allowance) has nearly all gone, so we are sending some of our wardrobe to the village shop to raise a few shillings, people are glad to buy anything in the clothing line but it is boots we are so badly in need of.

June 6th, 1942

I do hope we are not prisoners next Easter, even another winter would be terrible—the dark, cold, miserable nights of the last one I shall never forget. Some nights not even a candle to sew or knit by. The bellows were never out of my hand trying to keep a bright spark in the fire to see by. Now all the German vans, cars and motor bikes have been discarded due to lack of petrol, not only the luggage van, and that is a cross between Carter Paterson's van and the Royal Mail, painted red, with a door at the back. It is mainly used for getting the provisions from the harbour to the Headquarters. It was priceless the other day to see it stop at the chemist shop and three or four fat generals (or princes!) get out at the back, all medals and braid, reeking of scent. It was most undignified to see them after they had made their purchases, bundle in at the back, bumping their heads on the low roof and tripping over each other's feet. My fortune would have been made if I had been allowed a camera, one of the best pictures of the war!

The Island echoes with the coarse singing of the troops on the march. They seem to sing to order, you hear the officer give orders, then they burst out with hymns of hate, or so it seems to us. They sing with such gusto. Some of the Sark children and girls sing in German too. I never want to hear the language again.

June 14th, 1942

We have been without our wireless for some months because we could not get another battery, but there were lots in working order and we could go to friends and hear the news, but since the wireless broadcast, to tell the people in France on the coastline to get further in, all wirelesses have been taken from us. So now we don't know how the war goes on. We are told by someone in Guernsey that they are practising how to get away in six hours. Some more men

90

(fishermen) are reported to have got away to England from Guernsey and they have again stopped all fishing.

The detectives have gone at last and it is supposed that the murder case is quite cleared up, and no one in Sark involved, but they are such a cute cunning lot, they don't seem to let their left hand know what the right one is doing. In the morning of the murder a large batch of men left the Island for Russia, so suspicion may rest on some of them if the batman did not do it. There is another German doctor installed there, he is about twenty-eight and looks even younger, living in the same house, and sleeping in the murdered man's bedroom.

June 20th, 1942

We had a sad week this week for Dr Pittard died on Monday 15th. We miss him very much, he was a dear good friend to us for the last fifteen years. For some time he had been failing in health and his sight got very bad indeed. He got out into the garden two days before he died and sat for hours wrapped in rugs. Francis sent for me on the Monday evening about 10pm to stay with her the night, but I had not been there one hour when he passed away peacefully. The funeral was on Thursday and the church was full, it was sad to think none of his children could be round him at the last, or even hear he was ill. Ivor is in Jersey, but could not come over, Mary went to England for Betty's wedding the week before the Occupation and was prevented from coming back, so Ivor is alone.

As the time goes on we seem to get more resigned than ever to our prison life. Our garden takes up a lot of time and we are getting more to eat, lovely fresh vegetables and everything is quiet. We cannot even hear the guns in France and it is very rarely a plane goes overhead. We hear no news of any kind, except German news, so just try to imagine our thoughts about you all, the war, whether we are winning or losing or how soon victory or invasion will be. I feel our wireless will never be given back to us again. There is not one on the Island now and you may be sure the Germans will only give us 'Haw-Haw' stuff. The rumours are alarming and if we believed them we should be in the depths of despair.

We have had a Sark wedding today. It was Edith's from the Dosdanes and it was quite a pretty one, she borrowed Gwennie's dress, veil and orange blossom. There are no dresses to be bought in Guernsey and some say no wedding rings, so I don't know what was substituted for the ring. The wedding feast will last two or three days, they don't go to bed for nights. The bridesmaids and best man travelled in a pony chaise. In the good old days they always brought bottles of wine to the houses so that you could drink the bride's health, but wine is missing this year along with other luxuries.

June 30th, 1942

Eric's birthday. I wonder if he is thinking of me today. It is just two years since the occupation and I wonder if it will go on for another year. I sold a carpet sweeper this week for 17s 6d, another few marks to go on with, but I seem to be surrounded with good friends. Someone sent me a mackerel, enough for dinner for us both, and in the evening a basket of raspberries arrived and a dish of delicious curds, so supper was provided. Next day, while considering the menu for dinner a lady arrived with a rabbit and asked if we would accept it (Norah has been giving lessons to her boy). That did us for two days and after that a stream of things seemed to follow. I wish I could let you know all this to save you from worrying, for we had a Red Cross message a few days ago saying you were worried about us and had not heard from us since August.

July 13th, 1942

Cameras have all had to be handed in last week, some thousands of them in all the Islands and there is a rumour that bikes, sewing machines and all silver will come next. I can see myself digging another hole in the garden. I may send the sewing machine although it is a dear old friend, I had it for my twenty-first birthday, but the silver, no, no, no.

Another order to the fishermen is they must take up their boats and paint them red, white and blue, inside and out, or they won't be allowed to go out fishing, so we fear the invasion and a danger of bombing. They do get good catches of fish but the Germans take it, nearly all, they have first pick. Gates are to be erected at the harbour mouth as they fear submarine landings. A whole new company came last week but each batch seems worse than the last. This is a lot who have started to milk the cows in the meadows, after the curfew, so they get cheap milk and we go short of it. The awful scare about the Colorado beetle in the potatoes is bad, and special men have been sent over to spray them. What with pests of rats and rabbits in thousands the crops are all suffering but the greatest pests of all are the German troops.

All our beans, peas and carrots have been eaten to the ground by rats and rabbits. We have hundreds in the back garden and the traps and snares are quite useless. The cat is getting so lazy that it won't catch them.

A pound of tea is the first thing I would ask you to send me. How I do miss my cup of tea! Sugar is quite unobtainable and saccharin is 10s 6d a hundred, if it can be had. Eight pounds was offered for 1lb of tea last week and someone is asking urgently for a little rice for an invalid. The doctor in Guernsey cannot cope with all the sickness. Poor Arthur Baker, the postmaster, went away for an operation and died in Guernsey, he was only sixty-two, such a nice quiet chap. The MO in Guernsey has said in a report we are only getting enough nourishment to keep us going if we stayed in bed all day. We don't seem to have any energy and we get easily tired, so I am taking a midday rest in bed with a book.

July 19th, 1942

A beautiful Sunday morning. I went to church at 11am, Norah had been at 8am, but if you could have heard the row at German Headquarters as I approached, you would have thought that Hitler had arrived in the night. The yelling and screaming of orders was really frightening. When I got to the Manoir (HQ) I found three or four German soldiers being court-martialled on the lawn in front and the Captain, a good looking German, roaring and bellowing at them and looking fit to burst himself, a true Hitler. The poor men looked like whipped curs. I have never seen such terror or fear in any living face, it reminded me of Bill Sykes and his dog, only six times multiplied, and it made me unhappy all day. I don't know what they had done as I do not understand German, but the worst of it all was the place was surrounded with Sark kids, looking amused, and people filling their water cans at the pump all agog. I think it rather pleased the officer to have such an audience, one almost imagined he was saying, 'this is what you can expect later on, if you don't obey the German rules.' They seem to have us in the palm of their hand, we know nothing and hear nothing, and they don't mean us to. The silence gets on one's nerves and the rumours, always good for them, make us very depressed at times.

We have had an awful thunderstorm but the guns were firing and bombs were dropped at the same time, so one can't tell the difference between the storm and the reports of gun fire. They are bombing Alderney and Cherbourg. Some say our Navy was there but we live in a dead world, no news of any kind, only the German lies in the newspaper.

August 1st, 1942

These are some of the headlines in big print; 'Britain starves her ally'; 'Rostoff defeat, a blow to Downing St'; 'Invasion of Europe would be suicide for Britain'; 'Second thoughts on second front are now disturbing Britain'; 'Extensive fires in Birmingham'; 'Heavy raids in Middlesborough'; 'Britain's greatest weakness the sea'; 'Second front would be Churchill's wildest gamble'; 'England's harvest of ruin'; 'Fiasco of Duke of Gloucester's Indian mission'; 'Britain's grave shipping problem'; 'Britain has lost her common sense'; 'Britain facing hunger'. All these lies are constantly being put before our eyes. An awful German pictorial on a par with our *Picture Post* is on sale at all the shops showing the British defeats. If we reverse everything we see and read then perhaps we come near to the truth.

There is a rumour that the invasion of France will begin when the harvest is gathered. They obviously expect the English to come some time by the way they are so barricaded in their houses and billets with barbed wire.

The 6oz meat allowance in Guernsey last week must have been horse flesh, for the public were advised to stew it well. It reminded me of a joke from the North: a maid of Londonderry asked his lordship how he wanted his steak cooked and he answered, 'Go to hell and stew it' (Helen Stewart). There are scarcely any horses in Guernsey now, all folk have to foot it, even out to the country parishes, unless they have bikes. Oxen are being used to draw heavy carts and vans. There are no cups or saucers to be had, no pots, or saucepans, or brushes. It is amazing how we all carry on. Soap is still scarce. I long to lie in a real hot bath, with a whole packet of Lux in it, and to soak for hours. We get one candle every two weeks, how we shall survive the winter I don't know, when the long nights come.

I did not think we could have survived this Occupation for two years, and we have now started a third. The doctors in Guernsey are very hard worked. All ways and means of getting to see patients are cut off, no petrol for their cars, and very few bikes, so that there is an emergency hospital set up at the Castel, where patients are taken and all doctors do duty there. We simply dare not be ill in Sark, we have no doctor at all. It is amazing how fit we keep, considering all things. It must be the pure ozone!

August 16th, 1942

We have been worried for we have heard our King is dead, but after several days we have all made up our minds it is only a German rumour to make us unhappy. The bit of news that does leak out only upsets us, for how are we to know if it is true or false? It is so depressing.

We had two Germans in to look at the attic yesterday. I believe they think we do some signalling up there, but we thought at first it was to take possession. The old mill is taken over for a searchlight and all electric engines are taken there, and as it is near us we wonder if it is possible to have a light in the winter, that would take away one hardship of sitting in the dark.

This week £9 is offered by the Germans for an English sovereign. In Guernsey they are advertising for coloured blankets to make men's trousers with, the shortage of clothes is very acute. Please God, before Christmas something will happen to relieve the tension.

August 18th, 1942

A red letter day. I sent my opal ring over to Guernsey to a friend to sell for me and she got £7 5s for it. I am pleased, it will help us over a few more weeks. I also sent a pair of sheets and got 12lb of sugar for those, so I am very happy and have started to make some jam. I would not have sold the ring, only under great pressure, if I thought you or Norah would have worn it when I am gone, but opals are only lucky to those whose birth stone it is. I remember once when one of you wore my opal brooch you had bad luck all day. Awful thought, will I have bad luck because I sold it?

Each day something gives out and there is no more. I had hard work to clean my teeth today, there are only two whiskers in my tooth-brush and no more to be bought anywhere.

A German just back from leave said he met one of our prisoners (from Dunkirk) who complimented him on his English and asked him where he learnt it. When he said in the Channel Islands, he was fair staggered. We are not quite so in the dark, after all, for we do hear some little bits of news sometimes, how it leaks out is amazing, but we are told hundreds of wirelesses were kept back in Guernsey.

August 25th, 1942

All the place is alive with rumours that the British have arrived in France. Dieppe they do say, and the German troops are running about like people demented. Some arrived down at the harbour with their kits all complete, ready to board the boats when sent for them from Guernsey, I suppose at a given signal. The German Captain had a heart attack and had to be given restoratives. Towards the end of the day things got quieter and some of the barricades were removed, we were almost wired in to our gardens and at Little Sark no one was allowed to cross the Coupée even to come and buy their bread and provisions. We seem to be so used to the troops that there never seems to have been a time when they were not here. The harvest is nearly all in and we all wonder if the invasion will really come then. There is a splendid wheat crop, barley and oats and the potato crop is good, so half the winter fears are over. We are still hoping and praying that peace will come before Christmas. The Guernsey jam factory is giving 6s a basket for blackberries and the Sark folk are picking for them. There are tons and tons. The apple crop is not too bad either, so up to Christmas and the New Year they will fill many an empty tummy.

The curfew has been altered this week to 10pm because the French workmen in Guernsey have been singing their national anthem and God save the King. There are awful headlines in the paper this week, here are a few: 'Fiasco of British landing in France', 'Churchill's wild venture at Stalin's dictation', 'Churchill's visit to Moscow', 'Ample evidence that crisis is serious', 'British set-backs', 'Brave men's lives sacrificed at Dieppe in vain', and heaps more vile statements. If we want to cut wood or lop branches, cut gorse or get any fuel we must appear at Headquarters and see about a permit, which means seeing five or six German officers first. We cannot even go to the harbour to get a parcel or meet the boat and no one is allowed to go to Guernsey except to see a doctor or dentist and then they must be examined by the German doctor, so we cannot pretend or make believe, it must be the real thing. The hospitals are full in Guernsey and there is an outbreak among the troops here, throat trouble, so another German doctor has been sent over and an extra Red Cross base set up at Little Sark. The autumn evenings are drawing in and a fire is the best friend we can have, but oh, for a light! Last year was a nightmare and I don't want another like it. The Germans have reconstructed all electricity and telephones, we have no part in them at all, also a barge-load of coal from France has come for them, one hundred and fifty tons, and there is talk of another barge, full of wood coming for them, they get all they need. The village hall is to be taken over by them for storing all kinds of food, they are preparing now for a six months' siege in the winter, how nice for us poor souls living from hand to mouth.

September 1st, 1942

The mental torture from this German Occupation is becoming indescribable. Yesterday I felt very miserable and depressed all day, nothing could make me glad, only a bit of the daily reading. It comforted me to read, 'Yes, thou shalt see thy children's children and peace upon Israel', so now I know I shall see Judith and victory at last.

The troops we have here now are not too bad, still the destruction goes on and the blasting of rock everywhere. We have got more or less used to the shocks and noises and take them all as a matter of course. They had all their ammunition at Little Sark, now the carts and horses have been commandeered to bring it in to big Sark. They have dug deep down into the earth and erected a building just behind the village pump opposite the Headquarters, it is all stored there and I suppose will be destroyed if they decide to leave us in a hurry. If things are true, we hear that if the British had stayed another hour or two in France this lot were off, all preparations were made. The amazing part of it is we don't in the least know if we would be better off or worse if they left us; most of us fear they would come back and bomb us. They are a dirty lot, I trust none of them.

I am reading *The Autobiography of Margaret Asquith* and Lord Kitchener's advice to the British soldier, 'be invariably courteous, considerate and kind, never do anything to injure or destroy property etc.' But these are destroying property all day and every day and take a delight in it. They have always been what they are today—gross brutes, like Bismarck, vulgar, heavy drinking, heavy eating, strutting about as if they owned our little Island and destroying all its beauty. I hate 'em, all of them.

The weather has not been too good lately and the harvest is suffering. The corn has been lying about for weeks and some of it has been turned five or six times already. It has been a very wet month and as the wheat is our winter store it may be serious. A doctor in Guernsey said last week it is the tomatoes that are giving us new life at present, they are so full of vitamins.

The Red Cross have issued notices to say all messages will be stopped or delayed if any biblical references are made and series of numbers, or anything that might contain a double meaning. It takes extra staff in Berlin or Geneva to deal with the offenders. We have had no messages, we are told the Fuehrer has released all prisoners in Dieppe district, in grateful recognition of the way they behaved when the British landed there. I wonder how true it is. Here they all seem ready to bolt if they get word from France and we are all hoping that one fine morning we will wake to find the Island deserted.

The prison is full in Guernsey, so full that the sentences passed now on anyone must wait until someone comes out when their time is up. There is quite a crime wave and it is mostly for stealing food. I should think the little Sark prison is the only one in the world that is empty, so we cannot be a bad lot, and except for the murder of the German doctor and the batman's suicide, there has been very little disturbance. The German troops we have of course got used to. A brass band comes over every week and there are great doings outside Headquarters, an eat, drink and be merry sort of programme. They have great hogs' heads of beer and by the evening they get well seasoned. We hear them singing all over the place. If one remains out one is only asking for trouble. They are quite a generous lot with their beer and cigarettes to the Sark people, there are plenty who do not mind accepting them.

This week German news says, 'The Germans now striking at the very heart of Russia', and 'Preparing England for the biggest shock of the war.'

No one knows the torture we are going through, waiting, waiting day after day, each one trying to cheer the next one up. Most days it is difficult and it is only by sheer strength of will and the fact that I am always busy that keeps me sane. I still try to hold on to seven hens, how I feed them, goodness only knows, but they do produce a few eggs a week. I am giving them buttermilk to drink instead of water and they get a free run and plenty of snails and insects. Eggs are 15s a dozen in Guernsey and only for the sick. The sovereign is now worth £10. Guernsey has no silver, they are printing 6d, 1s, 2s 6d and 5s notes, also all postage stamps are altered, so history is being made!

September 8th, 1942

Like Old Mother Hubbard I have been to the cupboard to get or find something for dinner, but I found it bare. Just as I was puzzling my brains to concoct something there was a knock at the door and Mrs Falle from Stocks Hotel sent me over a beautiful filleted whiting all ready for the pan. Now, if you don't think that was Providence, I do.

For the last three or four months we have had no fat whatever, only our ration of butter, which is barely enough, but Norah went to Grande Grève bay on Monday and found a large chunk of mutton fat washed up, so she brought it home and I clarified it and 'presto', a dinner for the gods! The blasting in the Islands is awful today.

September 19th, 1942

We are all in great trouble this week, another new order has come out and all British-born subjects have to be removed to Guernsey. You don't know what we feel like. If we are all taken in open barges with hardly any warm woollens or big coats, God help us. Don't I remember my winter in Strasbourg, when I was well-housed, waited on and there were lots of warm things to be had, but after being three winters here, wearing and darning our poor clothes you can guess how I feel. Mrs Hathaway is trying to get some people off going, but she fears it will include herself and her husband also. We are anxiously waiting the news by boat today. I am glad you don't know all the conditions because it would make you more miserable about us penned up here. All we do hope and pray for is that our planes will see what is happening and do something to help us in time. There is something uncanny about the stillness, not a leaf moving and a perfect summer day. We all seem to be waiting to hear a death sentence with bated breath.

A real live German General and six of his bodyguards came over from France last week, swanking about the lanes in all their regalia. The result of the visit is that about a dozen more houses and bungalows are to be pulled down and erected somewhere else on the cliff. Mine is on the list, so we have had a man to strip it of all beds and furniture and we are now waiting for the worst to happen. It is strange but we have no longer any joy in our possessions, every week they rob us more. We seem to have lost interest and our hearts are sad.

The men look like perfect devils, they come with huge hammers and axes and work like mad as if their lives depended on it and they are bare to the waist and sweating like bulls and indeed they look more like animals than human beings. It is sad that the schoolboys are all practising and playing at soldiers, doing the German drills, the goosestep and marching four abreast, bowing from the waist, heel clicking and gloryfying in it. They have never seen soldiers before. The girls as well and even the school girls are crazy. Miss Howard, the schoolmistress, has cracked up and is on the verge of a breakdown. They wanted Norah to take it on. She may consider it if we are not packed off to Germany in the meanwhile. Mrs Sharp from the hotel on Little Sark has taken over the school temporarily and Miss Watts has Miss Howard there until arrangements can be made to get the permission to take her to a Guernsey nursing home. Sark evacuees have not gone to Germany yet, but those who have had the papers to go are very brave about it, though there are a lot who will probably be got off for ill health. This order only applies to Englishmen up to seventy years of age, and their wives and families. There are some pathetic scenes in Guernsey. Thousands are lined up there, but there is no panic. Homes and businesses have been sold and they leave their homes and all they have treasured for an unknown destination, supposed to be the Black Forest. After all we have suffered for three years and the low state of health most people are reduced to, it is the most devilish thing that could happen. We sometimes wonder if England has forgotten us. Perhaps it may end in our all being evacuated, then I suppose they will fight for the Island.

September 20th, 1942

Our little church looks beautiful and another Harvest Festival has come around. The Thanksgiving service was very saddened by a prayer being offered by the Vicar for the evacuees leaving for Germany and all the new-laid eggs sent to the Festival are to be hard-boiled and given to the people as they leave the Island.

September 27th, 1942

We have gone through a nerve-racking week, there seems a blight on the little Isle, we are all a mass of nerves. Our evacuees went yesterday, in the worst storm of the year and the biggest tide for forty years. I could not go down to see them off, my heart was sad, no one knows whose turn it will be next. The German Commandant says it is not a military order and he is very sorry it has happened, so it must be that fiend Himmler. All last week the first five hundred who were told to leave Guernsey were to be ready waiting on the White Rock. They gathered on the Monday and the boats were supposed to leave at about midnight. There were two cargo boats ready and the people were put on and kept in the hatch until the next day. For some unknown reason the boat did not leave that night. Tuesday night nothing happened and no one was told the reason for the delay. The waiting and the suspense must have been hellish, not knowing what was happening. Next day they were taken off and put into the Gaumont Cinema to spend the night, then even after that they were sent to their own homes and told to stay there until further notice, what a week of torture and distress for the poor souls, and some had sold their businesses and broken their homes up. There are three or four thousand of them to go from Guernsey and we are told thousands have had to leave Jersey already, it is a much bigger island and many more English reside there.

The saddest thing has happened here in Sark. Major Skelton and his wife, who were to have been evacuated, have committed suicide. They had been missing since yesterday and a search was made for fear any of us were harbouring them. They were found on the common, he was quite dead and she is being rushed to Guernsey in a dying condition. I suppose they could not face the journey to Germany and the unknown. One wonders how many more tragedies will happen in Sark. I am a bundle of nerves today.

October 5th, 1942

After three weeks of nerve-racking existence another thing has happened. There has actually been an invasion landing on Sark but so little is allowed to be known yet and the crop of rumours is just amazing. I reckon you will know by the wireless and get a more correct account than we have here. Last night after a very hot day, a thick fog came up and blotted out the Islands, at about 4am. There was an awful noise, machine-gunning etc, and some say a boat landed in Dixcart Bay with twenty of our men. This we do know, a lot of German wounded have been seen and one or two Germans have been taken away and some killed. I know this for certain, for last evening when I was going to church I walked behind a cart with the coffins, covered with the swastika flag. Yesterday the German troops got so frightened that the whole lot cleared out of Stock's Hotel and went down to sleep in the girls' school. All carts were commandeered to take evey bed and divan from the hotel. The schoolroom furniture and all Miss Howard's school house furniture was thrown into the playground and later stored in the little prison. It was such an upheaval on God's day. They are terror-stricken and I think want to hide behind the civilians and be nearer the harbour for getting away if things get too hot for them.

Poor Mrs Rondel and Elizabeth have had orders to leave their house at a few hours' notice. We have offered them part of this house, but no one is safe. Any day the order may come for us to leave and go to Germany. There are still more heartaches now, for the Manoir and all its cottages have had three hours' notice to clear out. All the troops are leaving their billets on the coast and massing inland, so these poor souls have had to scatter all over the island. Some had lived in their houses for fifty years. The Gestapo are still here, questioning everybody about the landing of the British. It has proved uncertain how many there were, some say ten or more now, and they must have known the place well, for it is so heavily mined and barbed wired. I am glad none of our soldiers were captured. This order for so many to leave their homes is a form of punishment, I suppose. The curfew is now from 8.30 till 7am. Also we hear Mr Isaac Carre has been taken off the Island, his son is in the Merchant Service, so perhaps they think he may have been one, but it is hard luck that the father has been captured. On the night of the raid Mr and Mrs Falle were awakened in the middle of the night by two Germans at the bedside with fixed bayonets looking for any likely intruders. It is hard to believe we are only eighty miles from Weymouth, the fog is very thick and has been for days, but when it clears I should like to see the Islands surrounded by the English and American fleets! I never thought our men would land here, it was a plucky, daring attempt. The German news says it was an outrage and that the Germans were murdered in their beds and those taken prisoner were bound and taken away in their shirts and not allowed to dress. Of course, we don't believe it. Poor little Sark must be well in the limelight if accounts are true, and I am sure you must be very worried about us, perhaps you are thinking we have been shipped off to Germany by this time. Eleven only went from Sark and our turn is not yet. Please God it won't come.

October 15th, 1942

We are told the curfew is to be 7 next month. We are all being punished for the landing of our men. The Germans don't want us to know what goes on from 7 at night till 7 in the morning. I hope our men won't try to land again because it can do no good and the reprisals are awful.

October 25th, 1942

The latest to be turned out of their houses are the Vicar and his wife and there is some talk of the Vicarage being blown up, it will be so near the big guns. The Vicar has been ill for some weeks but it makes no difference when the orders are issued. Norah has been helping them. Also Mrs Falle and the doctor's wife (not Francis). Julie's house by the mill (where Maurice Baker stayed) has to be all taken down and the poor people's life savings are in it. They have gone down to Mrs Reb's. There will be no more fishing, all the boats are brought up and no one is allowed to go near the harbour for any purpose. Last week a bull was killed for Island meat but it had been ill for weeks previously, no one knows the cause. A vet was sent for from Guernsey but he was not allowed to come, so it was killed and eaten, but we sold our ration, we could not face it. There is no firing in France or elsewhere and we are all wondering if the war has stopped. This week electric alarms are to be put in all the houses. The Arsenal is now full of beds as well as the girls' school and the prison. We are going back into ancient history for guns are being fixed on the Arsenal wall.

No more families have been sent to Germany yet, about thirty or forty are daily expecting an order to get ready. The husbands are already doing forced labour in the harbour at Guernsey and they are not allowed to come home. Since our men landed in Sark we are watched very carefully and sentries are everywhere with fixed bayonets. Every road seems blocked and we go miles round to get to the Post Office and village.

Some of the headlines in the German news say: 'British attack and bind German troops—immediate reprisals are imminent for such a disgraceful episode'; 'Sark is attracting the attention of the great world these days'. They also say: 'The raid on Sark has figured in the home news, BBC'. I wonder if it has. Another headline says: 'Britain will put 1,376 prisoners in manacles and chains'; 'Hypocritical act follows brutality at Dieppe and Sark.'

The latest news now is that we are to be relieved by Christmas. The Germans here seem to fear a big attack soon, they have cut down lovely trees and shrubs, they destroy anything that interferes with their line of vision or makes a likely cover for any of our men, if they should land again. Those lovely camellia trees in the Vicarage garden, all colours, that have been there for fifty or sixty years and are just one blaze of colour at Christmas and New Year when other flowers are scarce, are all cut to the ground and nearly everyone's hedges are cut likewise, no asking for permission or by your leave, they just arrive with a great woodman's axe and set to work like fiends, that's culture!

Two weeks ago when the craze was to smash up the bungalows, they took Mrs Castle Brown's beautiful one on the lighthouse cliff and erected it on the cliff, the Jersey side of the Coupée. Yesterday we had a violent storm which blew it right down the cliff, men and all, several are injured and one reported dead. It became a total wreck—this house of five or six bedrooms. Bedding, blankets, shirts, and other articles were flying across the telegraph lines, a most amazing sight. Sark was certainly saying, 'that will larn yer, coming to this peaceful Island',—they little know how the winds can blow in this place. However, it is an ill wind that blows nobody good, and it brought us enough wood and branches down to take us on for weeks.

October 31st, 1942

Another birthday has come round, making three since we were cut off. Surely there cannot be another one before we meet. I had eight or ten visitors to wish me all the best, folks are kind to me. Some of my presents include one candle, a pinch of real tea, a bit of flour, some knitting wool, aspirins (and one needs them these days), a dish of curds, and all sorts of useful tit-bits in these hard times.

Francis (Mrs Pittard) made me a little ginger cake, she came and had a cup of tea and was quite perky and bright but at 10.30 that night the Gestapo, or Military Police, stormed the Jaspellerie and took her off somewhere, no one knows where to or why. Since the Doctor's death she has lived there alone, quite happy with her animals. The penalty for being out after curfew is severe and it is now set at 7pm. Some days ago some more high officials came over again, landing with a view to raking over all the details of the Dixcart Bay affair on the 4th October. They are questioning everybody again about it, and we think that Mrs Pittard living on top of the bay must know about it, or have aided the landing. That is all we can think at present until we see her again, if we ever do. All Major Skelton's case is being revived again. They think there is a spy on the Island and he may have been on the pay-roll of the Government, but you would think as the poor man is dead all this turmoil and trouble would end. His widow is still in hospital but recovering slowly. We are being more punished in this isle than in Guernsey or Jersey. The curfew there is 10pm, ours is 7pm. It is a great hardship for us, especially as most of us have no lights and it is hours of misery.

November 13th, 1942

There is still no news about Mrs Pittard, no one knows if she is in Guernsey, France or Germany and worse still no one knows what she has been taken away for. We used to read about the Gestapo in Germany taking people off in the middle of their dinner and putting them into concentration camps, but that was mostly for political reasons, but to enter your house and march you off at a moment's notice, without any explanation, is a ghastly thing to do. No one knows whose turn it will be next.

Sequel (written in February 1943)

It is known now since we have met Mrs Pittard that our man actually got into the Jaspellerie and was with Mrs Pittard for hours getting information about the Germans and their quarters etc. She was asked to leave the Island with them and refused, wouldn't I liked to have had the chance. She tried to keep it all quiet but the Germans are like bloodhounds. After three weeks they carted her off to prison, that is why they sent for our Vicar and kept him in prison all night. She was supposed to have told him one or two things.

November 13th, 1942

The Gestapo are still here, also three tanks have arrived this week and more motor lorries are expected. Corrugated has now been put up instead of the picturesque thatch on the little Manoir cottage in case of fire. There is a sentry on duty there now. Luckily, houses were found for the inhabitants of these cottages. Some of them had lived in them since their childhood. No guns have been erected on the church tower but all church windows looking on the German quarters have been bricked up with red bricks. The Germans are terrified that our men will land again and take pot-shots at them.

We have had some terrible storms, the sea is like a boiling-pot and as we are surrounded by it our thoughts are compelled to be on it. Yet the weather is very mild. On the table, as I write, is a lovely bowl of roses out of the garden, as fragrant as in June. The rats and rabbits are still tearing about the island. It is a Pied Piper we want here to get rid of them, for they defy the cats and just sit up and finish their nibbling while you watch them. Dogs are not allowed off the lead, and most people have had to get rid of them because of the food problem, and so we go on.

Saturday, November 14th, 1942

The Vicar today has been taken off the Island, German orders. He is far from well as he has only just got over an illness and hardly recovered his strength, and no one knows why he has been taken. They had to leave the Vicarage as it was wanted for military purposes. They had scarcely got straight in the new house when he was taken from there. It all seems connected with the landing at Dixcart Bay but how he can be involved, I don't know. The church is closed today, no services at all.

November 23rd, 1942

Poor Miss Hale was turned out of her house this week, dozens of people helped to get her into another house, but she has so many things to move that it was terrible. moving at any time is unpleasant but if you could only get a bird's-eye view of these moves you would never forget it till your dying day. Every window was flung open and pictures, beds, chairs and tables thrown out and caught on the other side, if lucky. I am going down to try and help her. Meanwhile she is surrounded with boxes and packing cases, still as chirpy as a robin and as brave as possible, she is well over eighty. We are still in our house but for how long?

The huge Stock's Hotel is now quite empty for the Germans have taken away all the furniture. Some of the furniture was very old, the Germans will have every comfort, armchairs, the best of beds, carpets, lovely curtains etc. Furniture that has never left the island, oak, quite black with age, all thrown on carts and rattled along and tossed off just like common timber. The horses are worn out with work, they were never very strong or suitable, and they are working every day for long hours, even Sundays, so some of the poor beasts may drop dead soon.

Thank goodness our house is on the outside of the wire barricades. Since the raid in Dixcart Valley, it is shunned like the devil. I wonder if the Germans have ever seen the lady in white who is supposed to walk in the lane after midnight, when they patrol in the night. There are supposed to be several Sark ghosts, how I wish they would appear altogether one night and put the fear into the Germans. What about the monk at the Manoir, their Headquarters, who is supposed to tread the passages all night, at intervals, chanting music?

November 25th, 1942

Sark is once more in the limelight. A huge four-engined bomber came down near the Eperquerie in the night, luckily it was bright moonlight. It was ours and the three men left in it were landed safely, while four of the crew baled out in Germany and got rid of their bombs there, fortunately for us. The fields are so small here that it is a perfect miracle they were not killed or some damage done. It seemed to hover around some time before landing, looking for a place to come down and it was so low that it nearly touched the tops of the houses. The pilot must have been super to have landed it safely, the plane is almost intact and only the hedges affected. The pilot was only twenty-one years old, it seemed a great pity they could not get to England but their petrol had given out. More houses were searched to find likely men who might have escaped on the north of the Island. They were treated well, given hot coffee and cigarettes, then taken by boat to Guernsey, probably they are in France now or Germany. The plane is on view, it looks enormous and shines like silver in the sun. It seems a sin if they break it up, for only the tail is damaged with crashing in the hedge. Needless to say all Sark has visited the wreck, it is indeed a sight to see. Another two hundred soldiers have come this week, now there is almost a soldier for each one of us! They have taken the Aga from Stock's Hotel now for the Manoir, there was one there but they have broken it and have pitched it on the rubbish heap.

Our boots and clothes are still hanging together with the aid of safety pins, cotton and needles. Our rations are getting fewer, we haven't much energy so we soon get tired and as the days are shorter we are blacked out at about 6pm and then make up a good fire, the Germans have given us a permit to lop some trees at last. Our light is a glimmer, an ordinary battery for taking out on dark nights. We sit close together, huddled up and try to read till we 'begin to see red' then we make for the stairs and up to bed we go, knocking our shins to bits on the way. 'Ours is a nice house, ours is', and the Island too at the present time.

November 29th, 1942

Poor dear Mr Toplis died on Friday and is to be buried tomorrow. The old lady is bearing up wonderfully. He has had a most interesting life and his work will still live on. Unfortunately the Germans are trying to buy his paintings to take back to Germany. A German officer offered four pounds for one of his big masterpieces, they are not well off but will not part with any pictures.

All the dear old residents seem to be departing and Sark is no longer the same. I wonder each day if I shall want to live here after the war is over. There seems to be a curse on the whole Island, we are as much on the battle-front as if we were in Russia, spied on, robbed and punished in every way.

December 8th, 1942

Here we are into the Christmas month once again. I never thought last Christmas that we should have another under the swastika and even now I think a miracle will happen and we shall get a *real* post from England, how I long for news of you all, the suspense and loneliness is awful at times. Considering everything, our spirits are wonderful, somehow we seem to have got used to the conditions and hardships of everyday life and it has taught us many a lesson I can assure you. If I ever grumble again I hope God will punish me. I have sold blankets, sheets, linen, silver, china, beds and all sorts of things to keep the pot boiling and we have never been without a meal of some sort, which is a lot to be thankful for. How I shall ever start again to cater for guests, I don't know. I feel to old now and a lot of my sap has been used up. I am searching and asking everywhere for a pot of honey to give Norah for a Christmas present, but I've not been lucky up to the present. She is desperate for something sweet to eat, and says after the war she will eat a pound of chocolates right off. An advertisement in the Guernsey paper this week asks urgently for one pot of jam for an old lady's Christmas present, there are some distressing cases of want over there. Our biggest hardship is isolation and being cut off. No one is allowed to leave the Island or come to it for any reason whatever.

December 17th, 1942

It is nearly six months since I heard from any of you but we hear there is a record batch of Red Cross messages on the way. Looking through my Diary I find that I am getting less interesting and more tired, so I must pull up my socks and look forward to a happier year.

We know that Mrs Pittard is in prison, so October 4th has proved to be a sorry day for her. No invitations are taking place this Christmas, no parties, folk are just treating it as an ordinary day. The weather is mild and very wet, the roads and lanes are running with water and mud, churned up with beastly army lorries. More vehicles have been sent over after killing all the Sark horses with hard work. The poor beasts are just living skeletons—they are also suffering from lack of food, the same as we are.

All the quaint Sark laws are dying and one wonders if it will ever be the same again. By the time the houses and the hotels are built up and established, I shall perhaps be pushing up the daisies. There I am again, do let's be cheerful! If you could see the filthy mark notes being passed around, battered and torn and held together with stamp edge it makes me long to see and feel a new crisp £5 Bank of England note. Oh, let it be soon!

I dream of England most nights, especially Waterloo Station where many a meeting and parting has taken place. How is Judith? And do you tell her about Granny and Auntie Norah? I have tried to picture you and Norah at three years old, and the funny little sayings you had which she will be using. Who would have thought I would not see my first grandchild for three years? Don't say it might be four, I couldn't bear another year.

There are no cards and no presents to be had, in fact even very little second-hand clothing is to be had and no more boots. Clogs are being made in France and are for sale in Guernsey and wooden soles are being put into boots. Things are a terrible price, sheets, if any, are £3 and £4 a pair, blankets are £5 and men's suits up to £20, there are no towels to be had, we are using all makeshift. Goods of all kinds are becoming scarcer and we dread the boats stopping from France, for we depend on them for all our rations. Haricot beans that in peace-time were 2d a lb are now 6s 6d, think of it!

Christmas Day, December 25th, 1942
Our third Christmas under German rule and no boat from England

Another Christmas has gone by and we are still prisoners. The day passed over very nicely. Miss Mac. came to dinner and I cooked her chicken. We had no plum pudding or mince pies or cake, but we had a bottle of French wine, and all went off quietly. I made some girdle cakes for tea. We all seem more hopeful for the coming year and feel certain in our bones there won't be another Christmas to share with 'our guests'. They (the Germans) have been very quiet and orderly over the holidays. One went to Dixcart Hotel and demanded a drink (he was already drunk), and because he was refused, he smashed a window, but the officer came almost at once, had him arrested and the glass was put in by 8am in the morning by the Germans. There is a stricter watch kept on the troops this year and it is good for us because the previous Christmases and New Year it has been like hell at the hotels, but now the drink is scarce and not so strong, so it is well for the Island.

It has been a terrible year of suffering and hardships, a year of sorrows, many deaths of dear old friends, suicides, the evacuation of thousands of people from the Island to Germany, God knows how they are suffering there. People turned out of their cottages here, all our rights and privileges taken from us. How we miss our wireless, we hear that the German soldiers have had theirs taken from them as well. We know by the German newspapers that Darlan has been assassinated and that there is great unrest in France.

Boxing Day we went to have tea with dear Mrs Toplis and she gave us each a picture of Mr Toplis's work. Tuesday we were invited to tea at Mrs Robinson's. On Thursday we are having tea with the Vicar and his wife, they are in a temporary house and he is not at all well since his visit to Guernsey about Mrs Pittard's affairs. He was put into a cold damp cell for the night on his arrival from Sark on a beastly little German boat in a violent storm. The food they gave him was not fit to eat. Poor Mrs Pittard is still in prison. We don't know if she is in Guernsey or further away. Neither do we know exactly what she has done or said. The schoolchildren are to have an organised tea next Thursday. Everyone is contributing things towards it so at least the kiddies will get a Christmas treat. As curfew is at 7pm there cannot be much amusement after, but lantern slides will be shown and a few games played.

December 31st, 1942

Goodbye 1942, the saddest year of my life, but God has blessed me with good health, and I have always found something to make a meal with and a fire to keep warm by. So many of my dear friends have passed away and I miss them. Sark seems no longer the same.

I am going to quote a prophecy here, and if it turns out true it will be wonderful.

17th Century Prophecy
written by a monk in the Island of Gothland.

'Europe will some day when the seat of the Vatican is vacant, meet with a fearful punishment. Seven nations will turn on a bird with two heads. The bird will defend itself with claws and talons. The Monarch will mount his horse on the wrong side and be surrounded by a wall of foes. It will become a struggle between East and West. Lives of men will be lost, war chariots will roll without horses and fire-dragons fly. The sky will spread fire sulphur and destroy many towns. Mankind will not listen to the forebodings of God and we shall turn away from Him. The war will last three years and five months and starvation and disease will be lurking the seas for prey. The war will start when the corn is ripening and reach its maximum when the cherry trees are blossoming for the third time. Peace will be obtained about Christmas.'

Now I wonder if it will be true. God grant that it will be so.

January 1st, 1943

Welcome New Year! I ought to use a nice new page, but paper is so scarce and I am afraid I won't be able to complete my Diary of the Occupation if I do.

There was no noise of any kind last night, all was quiet on the western front. The troops are going about looking very depressed, surely they must know by now who is likely to win this war. They have big mail-bags from Germany and must know the conditions there, and the shortage of food stuffs. We see all sorts of vehicles in Sark nowadays, tanks, gun-carriages, motor lorries, motor cycles, motor cars, all racing about madly. A big arm lorry could not cross over the Coupée, so had to unload this side of it and load up on the other side on farm carts. That was a blow to their dignity.

What they are doing at Fort Gorey goodness only knows, but all the beautiful granite from the ruins of the Bel Air Hotel is being carted over there, and as the ruins of the silver mines are there one wonders if they are speculating and trying to revive them. Gabby from Stock's Hotel was scared this week. She took all the dogs up there for a run and only avoided by a hair's breadth getting on to the mines.

Everything is very quiet in the enemy camp. They (the officers) are constantly having dinner parties with turkey, ices, champagne and plum pudding, so we are told by the Sark woman who cooks it for them. How the troops fare we don't know, they still hang around the cookhouse door, with their enamel slop-pails to be filled with watery soup. This last lot certainly look like C.3 men or rather 3.4, many of them are cock-eyed, some knock-kneed. A cat had to be shot last week (it was very ill) and one soldier had three tries to kill it and didn't, so it had to be sent to someone else to finish (hence cock-eyed). A case of 'Are you hitting where you are looking, or looking where you are hitting?' They look very down-hearted going on duty and sometimes the officers give the signal to burst into song, but the song does not come from their hearts, it all seems false and they go shuffling along, not like our British Tommies marching. You feel like saying 'pick 'em up'. I had another tumble yesterday, talking of 'Pick 'em up' and came a heavy cropper. A case of a loop in the mat that my toe happened to fit in.

New Year's Day has passed and a few little gifts we received included two real silver half-crowns with our own King's head on to keep for luck, one for Norah and myself. What we do hear at the moment is 'The news is good'. The true British bulldog spirit cannot be beaten. Hitler's New Year greeting to his troops is: 'German people are stronger than ever in will and means to victory'; 'They have sunk nine million tons of Anglo-American shipping in 1942'; another headline, 'Britain's gloomy views.' All that should, and is meant to make us miserable. Strange to say, it does not. It has been the wettest December on record and Sark is looking very sad. Lovely meadows of beautiful turf, hundreds of years old, have been cut up and ruined.

I have received your Red Cross message telling me of the second daughter, congratulations!!!

I had a letter from Elsie (our old maid) this week, and she tells us of the news in Guernsey over Christmas and the New Year. It seems that everyone's tails were up because there were all-night parties everywhere, and everybody helped and shared their eatables. I suppose one can say there were even all-night parties in Sark, as our curfew is still at the ridiculous hour of 7pm.

The German troops are better behaved this year with no drinking or shouting in the lanes. They are not allowed to be served in the bars and they have to be in quarters early unless on duty. One night last week we heard a great shuffling of feet on the crazy-paving outside, and wondered what was going to happen. We have been warned not to open the door to anyone after curfew. Norah was just preparing to go to an upstairs window and call out, when a really nice cultured voice spoke in perfect English (the Officers were patrolling with them) while knocking hard on the dining-room window, saying, 'Your blackout is not sufficient.' Gosh! We thought for a moment it was our men landing again and knocking for admittance.

Still no news of Francis (Mrs P.), we fear she has been taken to Germany, it is very sad.

I have told all friends about the arrival of your new daughter, I feel twice a granny. It just seems impossible that we are in the fourth year of the war.

All our cupboards are empty now as all the food we tried hard to keep for a rainy day has been devoured this Christmas. All of us are praying hard for an early victory or release, but the Germans seem to be trying hard to stick on to these Islands, their first bit of British possession.

January 15th, 1943

The weather is mild. The German troops are all changing this week, more are coming, worse luck. Last night we were awakened by tremendous firing of all the Sark guns, Guernsey and Jersey as well, our planes overhead, probably watching the troops leave, such a hell of a racket all night. This morning all is quiet and peaceful, no use asking what has happened in the night, every time we ask we are told it is only practice, but the bays are full of broken wreckage and debris telling its own tale. Each new company as it arrives seems to undo the work of the last one. The tunnel they made coming out of Stock's Hotel is all being pulled down and is in pieces now, the wood and girders are wanted to erect another atrocious place on the Island. Clogs and sabots are well in evidence with soles two or three inches thick, but stilts would be better in some places, for the dugouts they have made everywhere, including the tunnel, are up to the top in water and mud. Heaven help us if we have to shelter there. One of the new company men arriving this week knocked at the back door and asked for a glass of milk. The poor devil looked cold and hungry, and said he was. He was no German, either a Pole or Austrian. He was very fed up and it showed in his face. He went into the shed where the man was sawing wood and began damning the war and Hitler. All the faces of this lot look gloomy and unhappy, if they get letters from their homes they are probably heavily censored otherwise they would know the state of their country.

There have been thirty-seven boats sunk, all sizes including a German patrol boat and the *White Heather* (the one that used to bring our food and mail) this week in the big gales, the wind has been too awful for words, trees down and lots of damage done. (The *White Heather* was badly damaged, not sunk).

January 20th, 1943

This week we have gathered in the garden, roses, red, yellow and white, violets, primroses, blue irises, winter jasmine, hydrangea, winter cherry, veronica, red and pink ivy geranium, winter heliotrope and lots of others, so you see there has been no hard winter yet, and we are all thankful because of the food problem and loss of clothes and boots. Frost and snow would have meant a lot of hardships.

Good news! Mrs Pittard came home yesterday, Monday, quite suddenly. She is not allowed to sleep at the Jaspellerie so I suppose

113

she will be well watched, but we have not seen her yet. Last night I dreamt I was in a sports field in England and heard them singing 'God save the King'. It was so real that I almost joined in when I woke up. These are some of the big headlines in the German newspaper: 'Britain and her Empire at the mercy of the Wall St. Jews'; 'Plutocrats crippling grip in Britain's mode of living'; 'North Africa another Dunkirk'; 'Britain's heritage the price of North Africa'; 'Roosevelt responsible for war'; 'German U-boats score terrific successes, 90 million tons of shipping sunk this week by subs.' So you see, all this constantly put before our eyes and not hearing *our* news is apt to make us feel down-hearted and miserable sometimes.

There has been a census of all the animals taken this week, pigs, hens, cows, goats etc, not a German order. Farmers have been killing animals and selling privately and getting enormous sums for joints of meat. One lady living in Jersey wrote to a friend here and said she had to pay £1 18s 6d for a 2lb joint of pork for Christmas, think of it!! There has been a lot of profiteering going on in the larger Islands, but the black market is at last stopped in Guernsey. The last auction sale was last week and made outstanding prices, here are some: ½lb of real tea brought £7 7s 6d; salmon 26s and 28s a tin; crab 10s and 12s a tin; ½lb tapioca 6s; one packet of candles 38s; tins of fruit 16s; one tin Heinz tomato soup (Woolworth's size) 12s; one tin grate polish 7s 6d; and worst of all, 8s for a single egg. In Guernsey they have at last put a stop to it all and quite time too.

Mrs Pittard has been in and looks remarkably well considering her eleven weeks in prison. She says she had good food if somewhat rough and was well treated, allowed to warm herself by a fire and choose books to read, and looks on it as a little rest and holiday—some holiday and experience! She is not allowed to sleep at her home, but can carry on there in the day time. The weather is still mild although the rain pours down in torrents. There is heavy firing from Guernsey towards France, cutting over the north end of Sark. So all the poor folk have to turn out of their homes from 9am until 1pm. There are a lot of invalids, some over ninety years old. Also a woman who has just had an infant must remove it and put it to bed again at the house open to take her in, also several others, it's ghastly. One old soul has been in bed (Philip's granny) for five years and she will have to be moved in an ambulance. Everyone has to clear out or run the risk of being killed. Perhaps the next order will be for the south of the Island to take shelter in the north. They seem to take a wicked delight in giving orders one week, then reversing them the next. At first, when they occupied the Islands, they chose

114

the best hotels and all the best houses (of the English residents who had left) to live in. Now these houses are all left in ruins, and they have turned out the poor cottagers and are doing the same to them.

There has been a batch of letters this week from the refugees who left for Germany, they all complain of the cold and ask for food and warm clothing. That does not sound too good, poor souls, taken from their warm homes here. They, or rather some of them, are in the Bavarian Alps and they say in their letters home it is very beautiful but very cold and they are asking for boots to keep out the snow. Well, as we are nearly all on our uppers, it will be very hard to send boots, and food will be a problem unless it is from someone with farm produce or who has a little store by them.

January 28th, 1943

Nothing happened yesterday in the firing line. We got up at dawn, it was a dark morning, to light wood fires and prepare for a lot of the refugees from the north. All I could make was some vegetable soup and some coffee to warm them up when they arrived, but we waited in vain. About 10am someone called to tell us it was all off and post-poned for another week, that is how they like to torture us. A great many of the people had removed their furniture and all things important and valuable to places of safety, and all of us were told the day before to get plenty of buckets of water ready in case of fire. But, to put it in a nutshell, they were going to make a target of Les Autelets, the rocks just behind the Seigneurie and it would have been no dud shells but the real thing. It sounds hellish but it is true. So we now have another week of waiting and suspense wondering if it will happen. A rumour came over from Guernsey yesterday that four nations had given up, Finland, Rumania, Hungary and some other. If it is true we are delighted.

The troops here all say they wish it were over. Two of them came yesterday to the back door and asked if I would sell some potatoes, they did indeed look hungry. Needless to say I filled their bag. Do not blame me for helping the enemy! I could never bear to see anyone hungry.

January 30th, 1943

Sitting quietly reading at 9.30pm when an almighty banging at the front door terrified us. Knowing we must not open the door after curfew we shouted, 'Who's there?' Answer, 'Sark Constable. Open the door'. After letting them into the hall they said, 'Will you please find yourselves down at the hall at 9am in the morning for a medical inspection.' Fancy an order at that time of night! The way he spoke is the Sark way of putting it.

Well! I did not find myself down there. The day previous I dropped on my knees and hurt myself trying to climb a high bank to avoid pools and pools of thick slush and mud churned up by the infernal motor lorries. Norah went in the pouring rain and hail and tried to excuse me, but the German doctor said he would send an escort and let me come the quick way past the Headquarters if I could walk with the help of a stick. Sure enough at 3pm the escort arrived. He opened the front door wide and shouted in the hall, 'Escort.' So, escorted I was. Gosh! Some of the folk I met thought I was bound for Germany. And so we live, hourly expecting orders and always fearing an order to get suitcases ready for Germany, that is the worst that can happen, and death, but I don't fear death. That would be preferable to prison camp.

Well, the medical inspection went on all day yesterday, of all and sundry, today, although it is Sunday it goes on, also tomorrow and the next day until finished. They must think they have got the Islands for keeps and our health must be attended to, to make good citizens. They even had babies in arms—entire families up.

Some of us are very uneasy and wonder if it is the beginning of an order to evacuate to Germany.

February 1st, 1943

The wind is howling at the rate of 100mph. It is simply terrifying and it has been like it for days, dare say we shall hear of some more of their camps and huts blown into the sea or down the cliffs. It is an ormer tide, and the fishermen are allowed to go by boat to the different bays. It is such good nourishing food and has been greatly missed. In peace-time we all went by the hundreds and gathered them in the bays, they were holidays and gala days of pleasure. It was a sight to see us in our old clothes and boots coming home laden with dripping ormers, wet through.

The harbour is completely closed to all civilians. Germans are working night and day there, no one knows what they are up to but a huge gate (portcullis) is erected in front of the main tunnel entrance and the new harbour put out of bounds and unget-at-able. What the end of Sir Lindsay Parkinson's work will be, goodness only knows. The men who were sent to Alderney to finish work there (German order) were told it was either Alderney or Germany.

There is a rumour that France wants to make a loan to the Islands and the Islands won't accept it, because they are bankrupt and have no guarantee. The new harbour in Sark was to cost £34,000 when finished. There is an outbreak of typhus and diphtheria in Guernsey and Jersey. Sark is free of it so far and I hope it remains so, some say the medical was for that, others that it was to see who was fit to send to Germany. The postponed shooting from Guernsey across the centre of Sark has not come off so far and we wonder if it has been stopped for international reasons for such a thing is not done in civilized countries. The officers from here have been called to Guernsey this week and we always fear them returning. We have heard this week that the Channel Islanders have been prayed for at St Martins in the Field and they appear to know what we are short of most. Surely a transmitter must be working somewhere. We also hear the Russians are doing splendidly and surrounding the Germans. The officers here still strut around too fat to move, some of them. It is a wonder their horses don't give way under their weight. It is now compulsory to learn the German language up to the age of eighteen, it does not seem to matter about the elders, it will be to join 'Hitler youth'. He has got some hope. (Hitler à la Mr Churchill). 'Some chicken, some neck.' Lots of sad letters arrived from our evacuees who have gone to Germany. Some of them are in huge castles, 600 years old, and it is very cold with lots of snow. The poor souls, after leaving nice comfortable homes, it must be hell for them.

February 7th, 1943

Another order came over on the German boat today, and about thirty or forty more are to be carted off to Germany, all mostly British, but a good few of the Islanders as well. All have been served with papers and told to be ready in two or three days. We hardly know how it has happened, but we are not chosen this time, but sadder still, nearly all our friends have been included and we shall be left almost entirely alone. There are heartbreaking sights everywhere, homes are being broken up, furniture carted about the Island, pets to be destroyed, cats, dogs, sheep etc. It is quite unbelievable that it could happen to this Island. Some of the Sarkees have never been off the Island before. They are taking our Vicar and his wife. The Seigneur (not Mrs Hathaway), Mrs Campbell, Miss Cheesewright, Miss Carter, Mrs Pittard again, the two ladies from the Dixcart Hotel, Miss Watts and lots of others are taken off. I am sorry for poor Francis, apparently they only let her come home for a few days to get her affairs in order, then took her off again, goodness knows where to this time. They have also taken the school mistress away, so Norah is asked to take the school on temporarily. We do not know how soon our turn will come, I don't know why we have escaped so far, unless it is that at the medical inspection our hearts were not found too good.

February 12th, 1943

Our refugees left today, I could not go and see them off. Norah went to the harbour but came back very upset and said, 'I never want to witness such a sight again.' There seemed to be a mile of them with carriages, all trundling along with blankets and haversacks on their backs, a small suitcase in one hand and enough eatables to last four or five days in the other, all trying to bear up, bursting with grief inside. The Vicar had prayers in the hall just before leaving and there were Germans walking behind the procession to watch no one escaped and a roll-call was read. It was a frightful day, blowing a blizzard at the harbour and a very low tide indeed. A huge barge or cattle boat had been sent for them and it was so low in the water that a perfectly straight ladder was fixed from the top of the harbour to below deck and all had to do the perilous climb—'yours truly' could never have done it. Another sad thing happened on the same day. The nurse who had been doing duty here (midwife) was taken ill suddenly and had to be taken off at once in the same boat to Guernsey Hospital (appendicitis) so she, with the help of the Captain and two Germans, had to be put on board by the crane as it was impossible to get her on the ambulance in any other way. Mrs Hathaway is taking care of her babies for a while. I think I mentioned that Dr Pittard brought them into the world, his last bit of doctoring. Before we all said goodbye to our friends they agreed that as they left the little harbour they would burst into song, and Norah said the tunnel echoed with 'Pack up your Troubles' and 'There will always be an England'. Someone thought it would not be too wise to sing 'Rule Britannia'. The scenes were bad enough here, but I believe in Guernsey it was worse, for many more joined them there and they sailed in a huge boat but not a Red Cross boat as it might have been bombed any time, as all departures are made at night and especially in moonlight.

The Vicar has asked us to take care of his silver, books and valuables, also we have been busy for weeks collecting the valuables

118

of seven or eight people, so the house, barn and bungalow are chock-a-block with goods and chattels. What will happen if we get our marching orders, I don't know. Well as there is scarcely anyone left, we will just have to leave them, there are too many possessions to bury this time as we did in the early days of the Occupation.

February 26th, 1943

Another sixty people are booked for Germany, thirty of them left today. Some of the Sark people were nine and ten in a family. It was difficult to gether together enough warm clothes for them, especially for the children. The poor dears think they are going on a holiday trip.

I am pleased to be left behind so far, but if I get a call, I know I will do my bit cheerfully and hope to meet our friends in Germany. There is a rumour that those already gone will be exchanged for prisoners in England and get there sooner than those left behind. Some messages have already come through and they seem fairly happy and say the food is good and that the American Red Cross is very good to them. Miss Carter says on the journey they had excellent soup, sausages and chocolate, the two latter we would give our eyes for. There is no salt here now so the cooking is very tasteless indeed, everything is tasteless. We eat to fill up and are no sooner full than we are hungry again. Every day seems the same as the one before, no sign of these troops going or, if they do change, others take their place and go on with the same devilish work of destroying the Island. We don't dare to be ill for a doctor is not allowed to come from Guernsey, and we wonder who will bury us, or marry and baptize, now our Vicar is taken away. Nearly all the clergy have been taken away in Guernsey. The Dean said he was unable to send a man over from Guernsey except every three months to do a Sunday duty here.

Every day seems the same as the one before. Typhus is very bad in Guernsey, thirty-nine deaths last week—supposed to be spread by the dirty foreign workers there. The bread is awful, some weeks we need a pickaxe to divide it, even the hens leave it. Goodness only knows what is in it, for it is almost black.

March 1st, 1943

How quickly this month has come and with it the lovely spring flowers and primroses everywhere. Without the garden I think I should go quite potty. We have very few Red Cross messages and I wonder hourly how you all are and when I shall see you again. My second grandchild will be walking and talking I expect and most probably Judith going to school. If we could only get a real letter of news from you all it would not seem so hard to bear.

The ladies at the Dixcart Hotel left us their dog to look after, a nice rough-haired terrier, and he is quite a bit of company but it is hard to get enough scraps to feed him.

March 11th, 1943

Another shooting practice from Guernsey across to Sark. All the people at the north end of the Island had to clear out of their houses by 8am. Those who had cattle had to be up about 5am to move them to this end of the Island for safety. Everyone was turned out of the Seigneurie. It meant many hours of hard work to leave their homes and then return about 2pm—six hours of misery. It was all a strange sight, particularly the evacuation. I have seen pictures of refugees overseas but I never thought I would see it here, farm carts could be seen soon after 7am taking valuables to a kind neighbour's house. Poor Mrs Toplis, Margaret and Muriel were turned out of their house by 7.30 together with the goats, Mrs Toplis in a bath chair wheeled by Margaret, and Muriel leading three or four goats. When they got to the Carrefour where the sentries were, the goats had a glorious time charging the guards. I suppose it was most laughable. The animals on Sark show some sense, the dogs cannot bear any of the Germans. Some of them may have had a bit of boot sometimes.

March 18th, 1943

We have had three or four letters from our prisoners of war in Germany, one says they are seventeen in one room to eat, sleep and live all day, straw beds and pillows to lie on, and they are surrounded with barbed wire like animals in the zoo. The schoolmistress they took from here is teaching the children there. The Vicar's wife writes, she hopes and prays we (Norah and I) will never have to leave Sark, so we read a great deal in those words.

March 25th, 1943

The prophecy says, 'When the cherry blossom blooms for the third time' a climax will be reached in the war. It will very shortly be out in full bloom, this year being the third.

There is heavy firing in Guernsey today. All the residents in St Peter Port have had to move out into the country while the big guns were in action. They are practising so as to be fit to meet our Navy!! I wonder !!!

April 1st, 1943

It is a beautiful hot day and there are flowers everywhere—cherry blossom soon be out. I am certain the prophecy will come true.

On Sunday the day before yesterday the civilian German Commandant went on to the lighthouse cliff to see a mine washed up, he had two officers with him. He got into a mine field, was thrown six feet into the air and killed instantly, his head was blown off. The two who were with him had to remain in the same position for about one hour until pioneers came to give them help, they dared not move. One of them lost so much blood he had to have a blood transfusion. The whole of the cliffs are mined.

Here is a copy of dates Miss Durand has had sent from her brother and it reads curiously don't you think.

1789 French Revolution	}	129 years
1918 German Revolution		
1804 Napoleon came to power	}	129 years
1933 Hitler came to power		
1812 Napoleon before Moscow	}	129 years
1941 Hitler before Moscow		
1814 Napoleon sent to Elba	}	129 years
1943 Hitler sent to ?		

I wonder if it will be hell!

A lady writing from Jersey to a friend here says she pays at the rate of 25s a lb for butter and a new-laid egg costs her 5s. No meat in meat form sold, they have to take jars to get it already cooked, so it must be horse. We continue to get letters from our friends who left for Germany. One says they have hot showers, baths ten at one time, think of it, the clean ones with the dirty ones, the letter says 'to be deloused' and they are, or rather were put into barracks that had previously been occupied by the foreign workers who were fairly walking with lice. Miss Carter has written for her lilo, she says she cannot sleep at night on the straw beds, and everyone is writing for cushions to be sent them, it is more mental torture, as if we had not suffered enough.

No more have been earmarked for Germany to date, but if there is any complaining about food or other things, they are instantly noted down and put on the next list for off, so, 'Mum's the word these days'. I have been out today and there is a rumour said to have come over from Guernsey that the 'British flag is flying in Africa'. Oh, if it is only true—the cherry blossom gets nearer.

A few hundred Germans had a tea-party on the Jaspellerie lawn the other day and a film was taken. The Red Cross nurses and marines came over from Guernsey to take part. They seemed to have plenty of all that they wanted, not a stint of anything.

Our rations are getting fewer, and the Island Authorities have been advised to get a three months' supply in as the boats may stop any time, but we would willingly eat dry bread if it meant that the end of the war would be quicker, but the bread is nearly killing us. It turns sour in our insides, and we are obliged to get medicine to counteract it. We were told last week that flour was being used that was unfit for human consumption, so it will be the survival of the fittest. The salt has nearly given out, what there is is like salt-rock, but when any is put into the butter or bread it remains unmelted, even after cooking, and is in big lumps, so that when the knife comes up against a lump it nearly takes the edge off the knife. Thank goodness the summer is coming and we shall need less food. The sun gets hotter every day so surely that will nourish our bodies a bit.

April 20th, 1943

Mrs Stanley Baker was taken off to Guernsey with appendicitis in a German boat at 3am in the morning. Also this week little Dorothy at the Mermaid had been taken away suddenly for an operation in Guernsey. Today is Hitler's birthday and they are celebrating with a big tea-party, also lots of wines and spirits have been sent for the troops so I expect tonight they will get rolling drunk and go singing around the lanes.

There is another rumour that, 'The French people have put arsenic into the wines and spirits for the German troops and powdered glass into chocolate.'

I have had another fall on my poor knees, don't know if I am getting weak, or clumsy, or it's old age coming on but it shakes me up a lot. It may be that we are all wearing boots and slippers five or six sizes too large for us, at present I am wearing size eight. Footwear is our biggest problem and stockings. Nearly all the Sarkeese are wearing French clogs, but they are big and ugly, and

35s a pair. Norah is looking forward to a week's holiday. She is not too well and very nervy. The Hitler birthday went off very quietly, surprisingly, not like last year and the year before. I never heard a single *Heil Hitler* nor do I think they hoisted the swastika. I wonder why. The latest order here is that persons may only send messages to their near relations, so that makes it more limited.

April 26th, 1943

It is Norah's birthday today, dear Norah, I sincerely hope her next birthday will be free from prison life. Other notices received from our refugees is that about twenty of them have to get a hot shower-bath together, under the supervision of a guard, think of it. And they are all hoarded together like animals with about as much space to move about, very little to eat, except the Red Cross parcels which they get every ten days. One lady writing to us this week says how she would welcome a glass of Sark milk and a bit of butter. We are lucky here and if we dare to grumble we deserve to be punished. I still have about six or seven hens. I try hard to feed them and they do produce a few eggs to supplement our rations.

May 1st, 1943

We keep hearing rumours of the invasion, and the mining of our coast by our forces suggests they are going to try and put the enemy to flight. A new notice up this week says we are to get ready plenty of sand, a pole or such like, to put fire out and a shield to protect against fire in case of need. It is said that the mad English and the madder Americans will drop incendiary bombs and we must be prepared. Also a notice appears in our local rag that Churchill is allowing the mines, knowing quite well it is cutting off our food supplies, and asking us people to blame the English if it means starvation for a month, and not the civilian Commandant. Another piece of propaganda, and some of the weak-minded residents say, 'Fancy the English allowing it to be done.' I would rather face starvation for three or four months if it means getting rid of the swine sooner, but I am sorry to say most of the very loyal people were taken away from this Island and the larger Islands, can't you see why? I can read them like a book. They were the ones who would most likely make trouble if a crisis arose.

Another rumour is that a real live fat, pompous General is coming over to Sark from France. No doubt more to be taken off to Germany. Some say women from ages twenty-five to fifty, so Norah is worried. I don't suppose they will study the schoolchildren or the schoolmistress.

Another Easter Sunday and our church looked lovely with lilies and primroses. It is a shame we have no vicar for the services. Some of the German officers came in and said how beautiful it looked, some of them apparently see beauty.

May 6th, 1943

A Red Cross message from you today, the first for some months, and we are delighted to hear all is well with you especially the two babies. So you have called her Suzanne. I had an idea it would be Elizabeth. I wonder how old they will be when I see them. Fancy, Judith will be three years in July.

The Rev Finey from Guernsey has been over for nearly a week. He is very nice, and by all accounts we are much better off than those in Guernsey. He was rector of the Forest Rectory which adjoins the Forest Church in Guernsey, but at the very commencement of the Occupation when the Germans seized the airport they took over the Forest Rectory.

A great deal of shipping has been sunk in these waters last week, cargoes of precious food coming to us from France. We also hear our friends who have gone to France are still at the temporary camp at Compiègne, Oise, and they have been there since February, but they are constantly being told that they are soon to go to a German camp in Germany. All the men under sixty-five went straight to the camp to get it ready for their families, so at present they are cut off from their women and children. I suppose the old French barracks (where Jeanne d'Arc was in prison) where the women are, is too dreadful for words. Miss Carter writes in great despair, she says, 'Aunt Kate horrid', meaning sanitary arrangements.

We have had a terrific storm here, quite unusual for the month of May, the wind is always in the East. We hear that Churchill is in Washington. In this week's news Lord Haw-Haw says, 'It must be admitted that North Africa is the first Anglo-American success achieved in the war.'

May 18th, 1943

Two or three generals have been over to look around the Island. All the fishermen were ordered up from the harbour while they landed and all the civilians were told to keep away from the main road and Headquarters for some hours. Perhaps Hitler has been over to look over his English possessions, I wonder? On Sunday two more Germans were killed at Little Sark—got on a mine field and killed instantly. It is strange no civilians have been killed by them yet and our men landed at Dixcart Bay where it is most dangerous, and escaped. The Germans killed were out looking for seagulls' eggs. So they are surely falling into the nets they have laid for themselves.

Another pathetic letter from Miss Carter, she says they are nearly baked with the heat, the only place to sit is in the glare of the sun on the barrack yard with hot clothing on, they went in February and it was winter weather, so all had warm clothes. She says the conditions are awful, and lettuce is 10d each, I am going to send her a boiling of new potatoes from Sark to cheer her up. We don't have to pay postage on anything to refugees.

A few headlines out of our local rag: 'Tunisia has served Germany's purpose', 'Great Britain sold to the Kremlin', 'Axis troops offer resistance till ammunition fails', 'Red Flag over Gibraltar'. I wonder. Photographs of Rommel being decorated and a whole column of praise for the hero. 'The Axis troops cry "no surrender" till the end of the war.' I am keeping all the newspapers, they are very laughable and amusing.

In the German news this week it says, 'Churchill in America has told them the war may last another five years.' If I thought it, I would say goodbye right now. Five months I might manage to stick, but five years, no!!!

A sack of flour has been stolen this week on the Island, the people are getting desperate. The detectives are here trying to find out who it is. Fish here is not rationed, we can have as much as we can afford, there is a depot and a fish controller but the Germans have 20% of all fish.

There is much bombing and blasting going on today, lots of ships have been sunk off Jersey and Alderney this last week. We have got to such a state here with nerves and depression, it is the same awful sameness of each day with no real news to gladden our hearts, only the German lies in the awful 'rag' published for our special benefit. I don't think we are so well off as prisoners of war in camps, at least they are allowed to write to England and receive Red Cross parcels every two weeks.

May 28th, 1943

More bombing this week all around the coast. Some say it is the beginning of the invasion, but I am getting so tired of hearing about an invasion that the thought no longer thrills me. I feel at a very low ebb this week and very sad. We are short of everything especially soap and candles. We are allowed one candle a month, but soap we have not seen for months.

June 9th, 1943

Here is a picture out of the German news, of the Sark harbour, these boats are laden with all sorts of food and building materials for themselves while a very little is for the civilians, but they delight in boasting of what they are doing to support us. I used to love the little busy harbour place in peace-time, it was all so quaint and pictures-que, and it was a real day out to go down and watch all the activity and goings-on, but now it is all barbed wire and dug-outs and ugly camouflage. A permit is required to go down even on business. Today and yesterday fishermen were not allowed to go out, it is rumoured that they are probably expecting the invasion any time, and the troops were ordered to keep their clothes on last night, so surely something is going to happen.

Today I spied a cookery book and on the front page in bright colours it said, '500 vegetarian recipes', so, says I, 'surely I will find a cheap tasty dish to tempt the appetite', but I have waded all through and there is not one that does not require nuts, bananas, apples, oranges, currants, raisins, cherries and dozens of other things we have not seen for three years. We sometimes take up an old magazine of about four or five years ago, and the tempting tasty dishes displayed on the advertisement pages make our mouths water. McDougall's pastry dishes, biscuits, plum cakes, gosh it makes one hungry just to see them. Bird's custard and dishes of tempting fruit!! Surely the day is not far off when they will come again. The bombing and blasting continues but we never hear where and what it is. We are living in a dead world.

Today we hear that the whole of La Valette has to come down, buildings, stables and everything. Poor Robert and his wife will be homeless. As you know the house is one of the forties and de Cartarets have been living in it for generations, it is one of the oldest houses on the Island and when we had rooms there over thirty years ago it was a little paradise. La Valette de Bas also has to come down. They talk about Sark being 'a pearl out of the necklace of the Channel Islands'. What it will look like if they leave, goodness only knows.

Two destroyers have arrived in Guernsey Harbour and there is also a barrage balloon. Serious fighting has been going on all this week around the Islands and live shells from the Guernsey guns have been whistling over Sark, breaking glass and scattering over the roofs of houses. Our huge bombers have been flying over, very low, and they have sunk a minesweeper off Sark and lots of ships in Jersey harbour.

Whit Sunday

Last week the vestry at our little church was broken into and the boys' surplices were taken. No one knows who it was. The Germans won't allow the church to be locked at nights because they have access to the tower where they can receive and send messages any hour of the day or night. Permission has had to be asked of the Commandant to have the vestry locked in future, and after a lot of performance it is granted. A permit has to be had for any trivial thing. The Island is no longer ours, and well we know it. Last week the German news mentioned the Islands as 'The former British Channel Isles'. It's German rule all right!

Whit Monday

No gaiety and happy parties like we used to have in the good old days on Whit Mondays. This sleepy little lane used to echo with merriment from 8am until evening (the first boat from Jersey used to arrive at 8am, lots more followed, also two from Guernsey), but the boats now are few and far between, and dear old Captain Hobbs carries his life in his hands every time he brings our provisions from Guernsey. Four poor Guernsey fishermen were caught in a minefield last week. Two were killed outright and the other two, who were good swimmers, were saved but their boat was blown to bits. A fund has been opened in Guernsey for the dependants who are left penniless and a concert has been given in Sark the proceeds to go to the fund. The fishermen who go out for our fish deserve the VC for they are open to all sorts of attacks from the sea and air.

Just heard Robert's farm has not had to be destroyed, it is to stand for the present as a result of a high court appeal, Robert and his wife are delighted about it. I heard this week about somebody complaining to the Commandant that her man on the farm was not pulling his weight or doing his duty, and the Commandant instantly said, 'Shoot the B. I will send you another man.' That's the type who would shoot us all for very little provocation. They are taking nearly all the best men to work for them offering them big wages. The women have to do their filthy washing and must not complain, and the young girls even of school age have all got swelled heads and are walking out with the Germans. Oh, to be in England.

June 21st, 1943

We have heard a rumour that our King is in Africa, God bless and keep him safe. Fourteen heifers are leaving the Island today for Guernsey, there is no food to feed them here. The Germans are daily roping the pastures and cliff-lands for military purposes. We are getting more tightly squeezed up in the centre of the Island with just enough room to exercise our limbs. The heifers are wanted for food in Guernsey, they are nearly starving there. I wonder how long this siege will go on, we are almost worn out. No sign of a Red Cross ship yet with food.

There was a large fall of rock at Grande Grève last week when a sea mine was washed ashore. The explosion was terrific, it shook the houses and broke glass for some distance away.

Another company has left the Island but more have come and they are not much more than boys who are being drilled in the fields close by. Meanwhile our Island boys are drilling and copying them at every opportunity. It is really laughable to see them if it were not so serious. Big black-eyed Tom Baker is sergeant-master and he gives the orders and commands in a regular German hard voice, just like Hitler addressing his youth campaign, same voice, absolutely German, and correct spoken German, for they all have to learn the language. Thank goodness Norah does not have to teach it. Frau Annie (the one who is at Mason's) had that job and I don't think it is paid for. All Adolph will have to do if he ever lands here will be to pop the Nazi shirt over their heads and hoop-la!!! It is no use blaming the poor kids they are just thrilled and tickled to death at the whole caboodle. Quite pop-eyed and just the age to take it all in. They have never seen a real English soldier. The mothers are not much better. They have the soldiers in their houses in the evening and the soldiers take the children for rides in the car, it makes us few English residents who are left positively sick to see all that is going on and we are powerless to help it.

A dozen U-boats arrived in Guernsey Harbour intending to make a base there. Our boys spotted them and one night reduced them to six. A few days after four more went west so they cleared off in disgust, that will 'larn them'.

'My horse's tail is gone?—Dammy! I had to smoke something!' One of Edmund Blampied's amusing cartoons which made thousands of Jersey people laugh.

STATES OF GUERNSEY.

COMMITTEE FOR
CONTROL OF ESSENTIAL COMMODITIES.

Your Ref.   LADIES' COLLEGE,
In your reply
please quote Ref. 88/2/1   GUERNSEY.

29th June, 1942.

LICENCE TO PURCHASE SOAP.

By virtue of Section 2 of the Rationing
of Soap Order issued by the Controlling
Committee on the 16th February, 1942,
permission is hereby granted to:-

MRS. E. RADFORD,
ROSEMOUNT,
CASTEL,

to purchase 4 ozs. soap during July,
4 ozs. during August and 4 ozs. during
September, exclusive of the amount to
which her household is entitled by
virtue of the abovementioned Order.

J. Griffiths

Vice-President,
Sub-Committee for Rationing.

States of Guernsey

Clothing and Footwear
Ration Book

FEMALE (16 years and over)

Holder's Name *Le Pelley Alice*

Address *Les Galliennes*

St. Andrews

Available from **January 1st, 1944** to **December 31th, 1944.** *If found return this Book to—* The Controller of Clothing and Footwear, Ladies' College, Guernsey.	Serial Number of Book— **№ 6647**

Signature of Holder ....

With such an acute shortage of goods on the Islands, everything—from soap to shoes—was strictly rationed.

Date .....11. Sept **19** 40

PERMIT.

<u>Schuetze   Bosserhoff</u>
Rank.   **Name.**

is entitled to buy .....1 Paar Damenschuhe......

in excess of officially fixed rations.

DER DEUTSCHE KOMMANDANT
A.B. *DER BRITISCHEN KANALINSELN.*

Lt.u. Ord.-Offz.

WOOD FUEL RATION CARD.

Heating of <u>Business</u> Premises.

Name *Priaulx Library.*

Address *Candie,*

St. Peter Port.

Coal Merchant *Messrs. A.E. Tory & Son.*

BANKS, BROWNSEY & CO. LTD., 250/11/41

WOOD	WOOD	WOOD	WOOD
1-Cwt.	1-Cwt.	1-Cwt.	1-Cwt.
No. **16**	No. **15**	No. **14**	No. **13**

TO-DAY'S LESSON IN GERMAN

NO. 121 OF OUR SERIES.

More useful phrases in English, with the German translation, approximate pronunciation in English spelling, and German pronunciation in English.

ENGLISH	GERMAN	PRONUNCIATION
1 Hold back your dog.	Halten Sie Ihren Hund zurück.	Halten Zee Eeren Hoond tsoorück.
2 Are you afraid of him?	Fürchten Sie sich vor ihm?	Fürshten Zee zish fohr eem?
3 He looks very vicious.	Er sieht sehr böse aus.	Air zeet zair berzer ows.
4 In my presence he will not bite you.	In meiner Anwesenheit wird er Sie nicht beissen.	In myner Anvayzenhyte veerd air Zee nisht byssen.
5 Then stay here or send him away.	Dann bleiben Sie hier oder schicken Sie ihn fort.	Dan blyben Zee here oder shicken Zee een fort.
6 I will be off.	Ich will selbst fort.	Ish vill zelbst fort.

Aussprache des Englishcen.—1 Hold back iohr dog. Ar iu efrehd of him? 3 He luks weri wisches. 4 In mei presnss hi nill nott beit iu. 5 Zhen ssteh hier or ssend him euäi. 6 Ei nill bi off.

Above and Below : Propaganda : items from the German-controlled *Evening Press* published in Guernsey on Wednesday December 4th, 1940.

LIVERPOOL IN FLAMES

" Liverpool is all ablaze." " Great fires in Liverpool " this is what the German fighters of the first attacking squadron stated on their return home of the heavy bombardment of Liverpool. The tremendous bombardment against the second biggest port of England, the huge centre of Great Britain's supply of food and raw material of all kinds, is continuing. The flames have only just been quenched in Birmingham, the debris of Coventry is still smouldering.... There are already the granaries and silos, the oil-mills and dry-docks, the petrol-reservoirs and the aeroplane-factories —extending for many miles along the Mersey-river in flames. The great docks

Opposite : The German authorities made every effort to clamp down on local resistance to their presence.

NOTICE:

LOUIS BERRIER,

a resident of Ernes
is charged with having
released a pigeon with
a message for England.
He was, therefore, sentenced

TO DEATH

for espionage by the
Court Martial and

SHOT

on the 2nd of August.

August 3rd, 1941.   Court Martial

BEKANNTMACHUNG:

FRANÇOIS SCORNET,
geb. 25-5-1919, zuletzt wohnhaft in
Ploujean (Departement Finistère) ist
wegen Begunstigung des Feindes durch
beabsichtigte Unterstutzung Englands
im Kriege gegen das Deutsche Reich
durch das Kriegsgericht

ZUM TODE

verurteilt und am 17-III-1941
erschossen worden.

Das Kriegsgericht.

Den 23-III-1941.

PUBLICATION:

The population is herewith notified, that
FRANÇOIS SCORNET,
born on May 25th 1919, residing in
Ploujean (Department Finistère) has
been sentenced

TO DEATH

by the German War Court and has
been shot on March 17th, 1941. This
had to be done, because of his favouring
the actions of the enemy by wilfully
supporting England in the war against
the German Empire.

German War Court.

March 23rd, 1941.

D7 HAUTE CROIX-
BONNE NUIT BAY
~~BRITISH VICTORY~~
IS CERTAIN

EVENING PRESS

 " La Gazette Officielle "

REWARD OF £25

A REWARD OF £25 WILL BE GIVEN TO THE PERSON WHO
FIRST GIVES TO THE INSPECTOR OF POLICE INFORMATION LEAD
ING TO THE CONVICTION OF ANYONE (NOT ALREADY
DISCOVERED) FOR THE OFFENCE OF MARKING ON ANY GATE,
WALL OR OTHER PLACE WHATSOEVER VISIBLE TO THE PUBLIC
THE LETTER " V " OR ANY OTHER SIGN OR ANY WORD OR
WORDS CALCULATED TO OFFEND THE GERMAN AUTHORITIES
OR SOLDIERS

THIS 1 DAY OF JULY, 1941
VICTOR G. CAREY.

Top and above: 'V' signs such as this appeared regularly throughout the Islands—they had the desired effect of incensing the Germans as can be seen by this cutting from the *Evening Press.*

Opposite top: Restrictions were placed on the number of postcards or letters which could be sent from camps. This card was sent by her husband Mr Robert Hathaway to the Dame of Sark from Laufen.
Opposite below: Dixcart Bay on the south-east coast of Sark, where British commandos landed on an unsuccessful night raid.

Interniertenpost
Postkarte

41

MRS HATHAWAY

Absender:

Vor- und Zuname:

N.W. HATHAWAY

Empfangsort: ___ SARK

Interniertennummer: 1348

Straße: SARK - GUERNSEY

Lager-Bezeichnung:
Ilag VII

Land: KANALINSELN

Landesteil (Provinz usw.)

Deutschland (Allemagne)

N/0017

A German soldier on guard in Sark.

The long-awaited Red Cross ship, *Vega.* leaving Jersey at noon on January 4th, 1945, on her way to Guernsey and Sark. The Red Cross relief expedition to the Channel Islands was an important and very welcome stage in the liberation. The cutting is from the *Daily Mirror*, December 13th, 1944.

Channel Isles food ship for Xmas

BRITAIN is sending supplies to the Channel Islands in a few days' time.

And it is hoped that the relief ship—a small Swedish vessel chartered on behalf of the British Government by the Red Cross—will dock there with its load of food and medical supplies by Christmas. It is already fully loaded waiting at Lisbon for orders to sail.

Thousands of Red Cross food parcels have been stowed on board. Five tons of salt and four tons of soap were rushed to Lisbon by sea and medical supplies were flown direct from Britain.

"It has been an incredible rush getting ready." a Red Cross official told the *Daily Mirror* last night, after Mr. Herbert Morrison had announced in the Commons that Germany had agreed to grant free passage to the ship.

"The Government asked us to be ready to get a ship away in a certain time, and we had to charter it, organise supplies and get everything in order without a moment's delay.

"Two voyages will be made to the islands, but they will not be the first of a regular relief service."

Altogether 300,000 standard food parcels, prisoner of war type, will reach the islands on the two voyages, and 10,000 invalid diet supplements.

War prisoners will not go short in any way, because the parcels and other things loaded have already been replaced.

Just as precious to the people of the islands will be the bundles of letters from relatives and friends. These have been held up since the Allies landed in France.

"They'll be terribly thrilled with these little messages," a Channel Islander in London told the "Daily Mirror." "Although they're only twenty-five words long, they'll spell out a message of hope for them, and bring them untold joy and happiness."

Occupied Since 1940

Two Swiss representatives of the International Red Cross will sail with the first ship, and may stay on the islands to help distribute the precious cargo.

The ship will be the first to bring relief to the Channel Islands since the Germans occupied them in 1940.

Lord Portsea, who is over 80, and has relatives living in both Guernsey and Jersey, commissioned a Brixham trawler

Above: The last menu for the German garrison of Mont Orgenil Castle, Guernsey, May 1945.

Opposite: The King's victory message to the Channel Islanders.

BUCKINGHAM PALACE

To my most loyal people in the Channel Islands, I send my heartfelt greetings.

Ever since my armed forces had to be withdrawn, you have, I know, looked forward with the same confidence as I have to the time of deliverance. We have never been divided in spirit. Our hopes and fears, anxieties and determination have been the same, and we have been bound together by an unshakable conviction that the day would come when the Islands, the oldest possession of the Crown, would be liberated from enemy occupation. That day has now come and, with all my Peoples, I cordially welcome you on your restoration to freedom and to your rightful place with the free nations of the world.

Channel Islanders in their thousands are fighting in my service for the cause of civilisation with their traditional loyalty, courage and devotion. Their task is not yet ended ; but for you a new task begins at once—to re-build the fortunes of your beautiful Islands in anticipation of reunion with relatives, friends and neighbours who have been parted from you by the circumstances of war. In this task you can count on the fullest support of my Government.

It is my desire that your ancient privileges and institutions should be maintained and that you should resume as soon as possible your accustomed system of government. Meantime, the immediate situation requires that responsibility for the safety of the Islands and the well-being of the inhabitants should rest upon the Commander of the Armed Forces stationed in the Islands. I feel confident that the Civil Authorities, who have carried so heavy a burden during the past years, will gladly co-operate with him in maintaining good government and securing the distribution of the supplies which he is bringing with him.

It is my earnest hope that the Islands, reinstated in their ancestral relationship to the Crown, will soon regain their former happiness and prosperity.

(Signed) GEORGE R. I.

PROCLAMATION

by His Excellency VICTOR GOSSELIN CAREY, Lieut.-Governor of Island of Guernsey and its Dependencies.

To my fellow Islanders of Guernsey. Alderney, Sark, Herm and Jethou.

I rejoice with you that the German Occupation which we have had to endure since June 30th, 1940, is now ended.

I ask you to remember that many areas, including the approaches to the Airport. are heavily mined. If you value your safety and that of others, keep away from them until they have been declared safe and be careful not to touch any notice boards or other identifying marks.

I ask you all to take great care of your Identity Cards. They must not be lost or destroyed.

As I understand the position, all stores and other effects of every kind and description belonging to the German Forces and their auxiliaries will automatically become the property of the incoming Forces. Any looting or destruction thereof will be severely punished.

For a short period the States will exchange German notes into sterling at the rate of 2/- per Reichmark but German coins of 10 pfennig and 5 pfennig will continue to be legal tender for the time being.

The various banks are closed for business to-day but will reopen to-morrow.

Every effort will be made for you to communicate with your loved ones overseas as soon as possible.

Next Sunday will be celebrated as a day of Thanksgiving.

This eighth day of May, 1945.

GOD SAVE THE KING.

THE END OF THE NAZIS

Surrender on Deck of Destroyer

A graphic story of the manner in which the German garrison in Guernsey surrendered, and our people passed once again under the blessed protection of the Union Jack, was told by Colonel Power.

"We had been in communication with the Germans." he said, for two or three days. As a matter of fact, our warships were near the Island on Tuesday afternoon. As a result, the Germans made an appointment for two o'clock on Tuesday. The rendezvous was off the south of Guernsey, and we understood that the Germans were sending a plenipotentiary to sign the surrender.

"When, however, this German did arrive it was discovered that he had no powers to sign, but had simply come to obtain our terms. He also said that, as the capitulation of Germany did not officially take effect until one minute after midnight on Tuesday, the presence of His Majesty's warships might be considered as an hostile act. Our force commander, Brigadier A. E. Snow, therefore handed him the terms of surrender, and our ship temporarily withdrew.

"A new rendezvous was made for midnight, when the German representative, Major General Heine, came out to the British destroyer Bulldog.

"The necessary preliminaries were soon complete, and the surrender of Guernsey by the Germans was signed by him on the quarter-deck of H.M.S. Bulldog

Troops Grateful to the Navy

Expressions of appreciation for the manner in which the personnel of the destroyers attended to the expeditionary force during their enforced stay on board ship at the time the surrender negotiations were in progress, echo from all ranks.

Particular emphasis is often heard of the many kindnesses shown with regard to comforts in the way of rugs and blankets provided during the hours of darkness when the ships remained off the Island awaiting the official cessation of hostilities.

Potato Ration

There will be a potato ration of 1½ lbs. per head issued this week-end.

GERMAN SQUALOR IN JERSEY

FILTHY HOUSES AND HOSPITALS

WANTON DAMAGE

From Our Special Correspondent

ST. HELIER, MAY 14

The collection of German arms and ammunition, the assembly and searching of prisoners, and the segregation of the 300 displaced persons in Jersey, including Spaniards, Frenchmen, and a few Russians, proceed apace.

Most of the Todt workers were removed some time ago, and Irishmen who were caught while working as potato pickers when the Germans landed five years ago.

This afternoon serious German hospital cases, numbering about 200, were evacuated from the islands. The very high proportion of surgical cases surprised the British. It appears that when cornered at St. Malo the Germans sent many wounded troops here. With them will go 19 German nurses who attended them very indifferently if the state of the hospitals in which they have lain in squalor and dirt is any guide. Evidence of poor feeding, in which nettle soup was frequently used, is reflected in the high incidence of skin diseases and ulcers.

The filthy conditions in which the Germans lived in requisitioned houses have shocked the dispossessed tenants now that they have an opportunity of inspecting the hotels and other holiday establishments, the appointments and fittings of which were wantonly destroyed. The Pomme d'Or Hotel, the newest on the island—its reconstruction was completed when the war broke out and it was the German naval headquarters—was found in a chaotic state and unimaginably dirty. Half of a dead horse, partly prepared for the cookhouse, was lying on the floor of what was formerly the reception hall.

Jersey airport has been completely freed of mines by German prisoners and is now in use for priority air transport. An R.A.F. machine landed to-day. Mines are also being removed from the golf courses.

The public telegraph service to the Channel Islands was opened yesterday. The Postmaster-General sent the first telegram, a message of greeting to the Post Office staff in

Above: These enormous 'pill-boxes' stand at the entrance to a house in the south of Guernsey.

Opposite: The remnants of war: this German field gun still stands in the grounds of La Seigneurie.

German marks printed for countries under occupation.

There is persistent bombing and loud explosions going on day and night all around the coast but we never do hear what it is all about. There are a lot of Poles working here and how they hate Hitler, they have good cause to, being forced to work for the Germans after all the torture in their own country. No wonder that lots of murders and suicides are happening everywhere.

In Guernsey every nationality is represented and they move about with all their worldly possessions on barrels and old prams, starving.

June 28th, 1943

We have heard this week that the Germans have taken over the banks in Guernsey, don't know if it is true yet, but if so, what a good sign that the end may not be far away, there is very little else they can do, except kill us all off. We have heard that our refugees have arrived safely in Biberach/Riss and all is better than the French barracks. Gorgeous air, 1,400 feet up, and they have met other Sark friends who left in previous batches.

June 30th, 1943

Our evacuees write from Germany and tell us what wonderful parcels they are getting from the Red Cross, it makes our mouths water, they wish they could send us some.

July 1st, 1943

Here we are, into another month still waiting for the Navy, how the months creep on and no sign of relief, I simply dare not think of another winter penned up here, with hardly any warmth or light.

We hear now that Churchill has made a speech, 'When the autumn leaves are here something big is going to happen', but we heard the same last year and it means so little to us here. When the New Year came in we lived for the spring and had great hopes, but alas! The prophecy has proved all wrong, probably it means next spring. I wonder! Grande Grève Bay has been opened for bathing but more for the troops than the civilians, lots of the Sarkees go, all those who have turned pro-German. I could count on my fingers the number of *all British* left, it is that chiefly which makes life a bit unbearable. Farmers are supplying them with milk, butter, eggs etc at exorbitant prices, asking them to supper and stuffing them with food that ought to feed the civilians. Norah is not a bit well, she has a very difficult task at school, it is not easy by any means. But there is no one else to take the school on.

The guns are constantly roaring overhead from Guernsey. Sark is a perfect target for them. Huge pieces of shrapnel are often picked up after scraps and mock battles. The Germans seem determined to stick to the Islands.

July 12th, 1943

These Islands get more fortified than ever, tons of cement are constantly coming over for some more of their devilish tricks.

We could do with more rain as a lot of the crops have failed. The Germans killed a pig last week and where do you think they have been keeping it? In the bathroom of that lovely old Manoir (their Headquarters), one instance of the way they are wrecking and treating people's property, what those who went to England will have left to come back to, I do not know. What will happen to us before the swines clear out, no one knows. How will they treat us if they have to leave?

We hear that an MP has made a speech in the House, asking for a boat and food to be sent to us and that Churchill has refused. We wonder why? It seems strange to us all that we are, or seem to be, forgotten by our own people. Some day I know it will all be made clear to us but can you wonder that now it makes us feel bitter and down-hearted. Added to that, the enemy is making the most of it in the German news saying England, and Churchill in particular, want to starve us out.

I am reading a book where someone is telling about a breakfast they have just partaken of, 'two slices of ham, two poached eggs, fruit, toast and marmalade and a pot of *real tea*'. Gosh for the tea and marmalade I would exchange anything!

The German officers have put the hard tennis courts in good order (those Mr Ladler made at 'Varouque') and they play quite regularly. They seem bored to tears on the little Island, no amusements or anything to take their fancy, only the Island girls and they have their heads entirely turned by the attentions they are receiving, and the way the girls are all playing up to them is really too disgusting for words. It's even the young girls at school that are tainted, it makes Norah sick. Where do you think the Germans tether their horses while playing tennis—in the old cemetery among the gravestones. It is a wonder some of the old folk don't rise up.

The people are taking an eager delight in using the German language, it is amazing, the kids as well as grown-ups. The strides they are making, you hear quite little kids talking it in the shops and the lanes. It really is a strange little Island at the present time, you can hear German spoken, French, Patois and English, there are Poles, Italians, Austrians, almost every nationality is represented.

July 24th, 1943

One night last week the officers, four or five of them, got drunk at the Vieux Clos, and smashed all the furniture and broke all the windows, then to cool their brains, got the car out and drove around and around the Island calling at various houses to share more drinks. What a glorious chance that would have been for our men to have landed and taken possession of the Island! If only I could have got a message out.

We are not sorry to see the last Commandant go. The new one seems much saner but more strict. The little Commandant has come back again, this is for the third time, but each time he has been, some sad thing has happened. He was here when the murder of Dr Goebels at the 'Vieux Clos' and the suicides took place, and also Skelton's suicide and the landing of our men at Dixcart and the killing of German troops.

We all feel a bit more hopeful this week, scraps of news come through saying we are doing well, although this German rag is full of boast and brag and, if we believed it, England would be no more, completely defeated, but never in our darkest hour have I believed this. I found a tiny scrap of red, white and blue ribbon the other day so I am going to make a rosette for the happy day and pray it is not too far off.

The swallows have built in the barn again this year, and yesterday I was nearly struck in the eye by one coming out swiftly as I opened the door. My brood of early chicks only three months old are nearly full grown so I shall have some winter eggs.

This is Sunday and it is very peaceful and quiet. One of the German Commandants, who has just arrived for the first time in Sark, has been in Russia since '41 and he says Sark is the only peaceful spot in the world. People who have been used to having the best in Russia are now reduced to going about with rags tied around their feet for shoes. It must be dreadful.

Alderney was heavily bombed yesterday by our planes. If we could only take Alderney and make it a base it might scare the blighters away. Talk says the men have been taken off the Casquettes several times, there are hardly any civilians living there, everyone was evacuated, so bombing would do no harm there.

July 27th, 1943

We heard this morning that Mussolini has resigned and Italy refuses to fight. I don't know how much of it is true. At last we can see the end in view. They were told in Guernsey last week to pull down all flagstaffs, so it would appear that they don't want to see the Union Jack flying. In Sark they pulled down all the flagstaffs months ago to light their fires with. When the first lot arrived they flew the swastika, but as the days went by, they saw how unsafe if would be with our planes coming so low to spy out the land, so it was removed. Even on Hitler's birthday this year it was not hoisted.

August 1st, 1943

The heat has been awful this last week or so and such a lot of sea fogs. Norah is lazing about in the garden as she has five weeks' holiday from school. The garden is looking beautiful, in fact a German officer's servant came the other day and said he wanted some flowers to decorate his officer's table with. Of course, we gave him some. Do I hear you saying, 'helping the enemy again.' They are top dogs now but wait a bit!

We hear that the Russians are doing well and Sicily nearly finished, also that Mussolini is in prison. The German news tells us that 'Germany relies on her strength alone', so by that, we judge that the two countries have split, lots of things may happen in a few weeks to gladden our hearts.

We have a ration of 2lb of sugar each for jam-making, and we both feel we have had a birthday present. It is the only time I have wished I had a houseful of children, for even infants get the 2lb. What a lot of jam I could make if I had ten children. The blackberries are coming along fine but apples are few this year. All our best places for picking blackberries are heavily mined and barbed wired, trenches, gun emplacements etc. The Gouliot is completely disfigured, that is where we could pick quarts in a few minutes.

August 2nd, 1943

Another Bank Holiday and the Island is very quiet. By order of the German Commandant we are to have an increased bread ration. He says, 'as there has been no interference recently with the importation of supplies by enemy action against the route to the Channel Isles, the rations will be restored to their former level from August 1st.' I must tell you that their former level was not too good.

The pictures and films shown in Guernsey (with English sub-titles) are all about our reverses, and the sinking of our ships. If we believed the notices that enormous tons of shipping are sunk each week I should think it would amount to more than we ever possessed. This week, 57,000 tons of English and American.

Norah may have to go over and have a tooth out in Guernsey, and she dreads the sea passage. There are so many mines and what used to take one hour now takes two and a half.

August 12th, 1943

Today all of us in this valley had an order to evacuate for three or four hours while heavy firing went on, so we had to turn out with a scanty breakfast, munching some of it on the way, to a friend's home on the other side of the Island, and there wait until it suited them to stop firing. When we did return, it was to find a huge hole in the roof of Dixcart farmhouse, quite enough to kill two or three people if they had stayed in their homes. The fact is these Germans, the latest to arrive are just raw recruits, don't even look as though they have ever handled a gun before, they fire fifty or more yards short of their targets.

The troops are still bathing in great numbers at Grande Grève, wearing nothing more than loin cloths, their bodies are a mahogany colour, Sundays mostly. About twelve or fifteen opened our front gate and prepared to come down the path while we were quietly resting on Sunday afternoon (quite ignoring the sidepath), but Joey, the dog we are taking care of, made a bee-line for the gate and it was lucky they got away with loin cloths intact, they looked like a lot of savage Indians. Our garden is peaceful, it is the only place where one can feel away from the troubles of the Island and the world, although barbed wire still surrounds. Perhaps this is the calm before the storm.

Sunday August 22nd, 1943

It is our Harvest Thanksgiving again and the church is laden with every sort of vegetable, a wonderful sight, and all of the goods are going to be auctioned, the proceeds going to the King George Fund for Fishermen.

August 26th, 1943

Five more people have got away from Guernsey to England in a boat, so we are all to be punished again. Fishing is all stopped and the curfew is altered. The fishermen are very distracted. It is the best season of the year especially for mackerel which they can now get in thousands, and this is the time they can be dried and kippered for use in winter. Then the conger begins next month, so they are likely to lose that too. It is useless for them to say, 'Sark is not the offender', all Islands are punished alike. All the boats and lobster-pots have to be pulled up. They punish us by cutting our food supply.

Norah went to Guernsey with her toothache yesterday. It meant three or four visits to the Commandant for a permit. It is very dangerous to cross at present unless absolutely necessary. Last night at 6pm there was a heavy raid on Guernsey Harbour and Airport, one of our planes was shot down in flames off Herm. Lots of German troops crossed at the same time, so it was quite liable to be shot at any minute by our planes. The German troops all get into lifebelts at once, but strange to say any civilians who are on board never trouble to do so—'British bulldog courage'. It is a huge tugboat, filthy dirty, nowhere to sit, only on the deck, so it is open to all from the skies.

We have heard that King Boris has been killed and wonder how and what effect it will have on the war. All the young German troops are being called up from the four Islands and older men sent in their places, men who have returned from Russia. Also thousands of Spanish workers in the Islands have been shipped off and we hear Spain is anxious.

September 1st, 1943

Norah says, 'No more Guernsey until after the war'. She set off on a rough day, and when she arrived at the harbour found it was the German tug (a troop carrier) and seventy or eighty troops waiting to get on board all in full kit, a roll-call was then made and all the men

150

given a stiff brandy—they needed it for they were bound for Russia. Then they set off with two swastikas flying. The Captain asked the womenfolk to keep near the wheel-house in case of planes overhead, so that they could easily get under cover, but they arrived without mishap. On reaching Guernsey she was well searched, all her goods and chattels showered about, then before she reached the weigh-bridge was stopped several times by German officers to see her permit, have it endorsed and so on. But coming back was awful. The boat was scheduled to leave White Rock at 2pm Saturday, but when she arrived to catch it she was told it was too rough and it would not sail until Sunday morning at 7am. Sunday morning she was up at 5am and got to the pier well in time, it was still cold and stormy, only to be told the German troops would cross, but no civilians, and to come back at 3 in the afternoon. All her rations for her stay were eaten but she happened to spy a friend who took her to her flat and gave her warm coffee and let her stay there until the afternoon. However, the next time she was lucky, only it left at 5pm still in the company of seventy troops and she was violently sick on the crossing. The lot she travelled with looked war-weary and they were older, gunboats escorted them either side and one in front all the way. There are huge holes in the roads in Guernsey, especially at Cobo, which they mean to fill with dynamite should the British make a landing, also on the White Rock, under all those massive cranes, they are all ready to be blown up at a moment's notice.

We now know it was not our plane that was shot down last week, but three German ones, shot down by the Germans themselves. The Germans who fired the shots have been taken prisoner and taken off in handcuffs. Norah says it is deplorable in Guernsey at present with Russians, Jews, Niggers, Americans, Italians, Poles and Swedes.

The punishment for the men getting away still hangs over us, no fishing is allowed yet and the sea at the present time is teaming with fish, the waters are quite iridescent, but we go short of the good fish. No fisherman is allowed out who has relatives or children in England, no unmarried man allowed to go, only men over fifty must go and if a permit comes through from France that will only mean about five or six to fish for Guernsey and Sark.

September 5th, 1943

I dreamt last night all the troops were leaving Guernsey and how happy I felt until I woke. All seems very still and tense, like one is expecting an explosion any moment. A notice in our German news says, 'if any civilians have guns etc. and they are handed in at once, there will be no punishment.' If anyone goes to Alderney, they must first go to St Malo.

September 11th, 1943

We hear that Italy has come in with us and we hope for great things happening now. There was an awful noise in the Channel last night.

I have often said in fun, 'Sark is off the map', and we certainly feel it now. The fishermen are still idle. The newspaper this week says, 'Mussolini has been found', and there is such rejoicing over it, with life-size photographs of him and Hitler as well. We think the news sounds good for us because we always reverse what we read.

September 21st, 1943

A large convoy has been sunk off L'Etac, six or seven hundred troops are lost and lots of guns and ammunition on the way to France. The Germans are leaving this Island in great numbers and don't seem to be replacing them. But we are all so tired of rumours.

At present we have plentiful pickings of mushrooms and blackberries, sloes as well, but no gin. In Guernsey, sloes are selling in the market for 10d and 1s a lb, grapes come over in large quantities but they are 2s and 2s 6d a lb. Tomatoes are not quite so plentiful, they are clearing the glasshouses for planting early potatoes. We keep fairly well, considering all. Norah is better than she was before going to Guernsey and having teeth out, she has less headache and is taking a good nerve tonic to brace her up for taking school.

We had a letter from Miss Carter in Germany yesterday, they are all well, and fairly contented, what's the use of kicking against the traces, we all know it's for the duration and it's up to us all to do the best we can and be cheerful, but, oh, the monotony of it all and signs of going into another winter.

The rats and the rabbits still plague the Island, I don't know how we shall be rid of them. They are eating all the potatoes and we think there will be no more potatoes in another month's time.

September 30th, 1943

A Red Cross letter from Mrs Lees today, such a comforting one. They were some of the nicest of our guests in peace-time. It has taken nearly six months to come, perhaps by the time they get the reply we shall be free.

One hundred and fifty German troops left the Island this week and 1,800 from Guernsey and have not been replaced. We wonder what it means. A Pole who is working here said, 'We are Poles and want to fight for England and the war to cease.' Our rations this week came to 1s 9d, 1oz of coffee, 1oz of salt and a little washing soda, all to last two weeks!!

October 3rd, 1943

The weather is cold but clear and crisp. A lot more German troops have left the Island and all the Sark and Guernsey men, working for the Germans, have been discharged. It all looks very hopeful and we feel any day now we may have a joyful surprise, we hear only forty troops are to be kept on Sark.

Headlines in the *Guernsey Rag* this week are: 'Britain's most grievous sacrifices lie ahead'; 'Disillusion for those who hoped war neared the end'; 'Germany holds trump card on all fronts'; 'Germany's strategic plan will make Red Army pay the price.' And lots more rot like this. We also hear news from Guernsey that German battleships have been scuttled off Norway. Another good sign for us and we hope it is true. My pound of English tea gets closer! These are a few of the prices here at present: one piece of toilet soap £6 14s 7d; one bar of Lifebuoy £8 10s; 2oz of real tea £5 6s 10d; three eggs £2 14s 10d; ½lb butter £1 0s 3d; 1oz of pepper £1 6s 8d; one reel of cotton £1 2s 4d; two candles 11s 6d. Think of it!!

News came over from Guernsey that we are doing well and a second front will soon be started. All is painfully quiet here, no hammering, shooting or marching and many are leaving every day, there is only one Commandant left in charge. Masses of food and furniture is being shipped now to Germany.

October 17th, 1943

A lady from Sark has just been over to Guernsey for ten days and stayed opposite Lovells storehouse and she says the Germans never stopped taking the furniture away in vans from the store to the White Rock, where they have special sheds and packers for shipping to Germany. What they are taking mostly belongs to those who left for England, who had stored it for safety (!), or so they thought.

Guernsey is like a dead city, all the shops are empty, most of them have shavings or coloured papers in the windows to try and keep up appearances.

October 20th, 1943

Headlines, 'Italy (the King of) has declared them to be in a state of war with Germany as from October 12th'. This will strike students of history as a strange and remarkable procedure. (So if the Germans publish it, the news must be true). Lord Haw-Haw (William Joyce) contributes to these wicked lies and sarcasms. 'Germany's food problem better than in 1939', (that's because they have robbed so many countries); 'Germany can endure no matter how long the war lasts'; 'Churchill sells his birthright to the Soviets'; 'Stalin's cunning design to sacrifice Britain.'

On Friday evening 750 German troops left Guernsey and 600 Italians (workers) arrived, also there are hundreds of Russians. Here on Sark there are very few Germans left, they are removing guns, tanks, ammunition and all sorts. These last three years have been a great test, but I know there are hundreds who are suffering more than we are in our sister Islands.

October 31st, 1943, All Hallows' Eve

My birthday—three score and ten today.

Here I am again, fourth birthday under the swastika and German rule. I am having a wonderful day.

A kind lady made a cake for me. I made some pancakes (the flour was a bit mousy but I put a bit extra carbonate in it to counteract it). Had five people to tea and two to supper. These are some of my presents—Norah gave me some wonderful flowers, another lady brought me a basket containing potatoes, carrots, onions, cabbage, leeks. Another gave me two candles, a few knobs of sugar, a little bit of flour and one rabbit. And best of all on my birthday a Red Cross message came from Ivor, and in it photos of my two little grandchildren, Judith and Suzanne. We shall be able to tell them they made history, by first of all going to Germany being censored before coming to me.

It is very strange because those people who were sent to Biberach and Laufen are having all sorts of luxuries to eat and to wear, and they all wish they could send something to us who were left behind. Cigarettes are to be allowed to be sent, I think, to their friends here. This is what Miss Carter has written this week, things she has had sent from Red Cross. A thick warm rug, two pairs of pyjamas, elastic, chocolate, Sunlight soap. Heating and they need it, towels, scarves, shoes, stockings, gloves, winter coats and warm frocks. She says 'God Bless the Red Cross'. I should say so. We poor souls have struggled on for four or five years and our clothes are all in tatters, the least said about shoes and stockings the better. We have been on our uppers for months now and not a single Red Cross parcel to us, poor Sark is quite forgotten.

My Diary does not seem so up to date or amusing lately, we are all getting a bit tired and weary. Also the winter is facing us, and the thought of another lonely Christmas. I did think last Christmas was the last one we would have under German rule, but here we are into November. There is no bombing going on at all now. Advocate Chervil (now a prisoner in Germany) wrote to the Bishop of Winchester to see if he could do something about our airports and not to bomb ships coming from France carrying our food supplies (German suppliers as well), as we are punished here when it happens and our rations considerably shortened and, goodness knows, they are short enough, if you could see what we get to last a week!

Miss McEwan came in yesterday, she had nearly passed out experimenting with some of the rations. We had a bag of something that looked like beautiful white flour, and as it is ages since we saw it, the sight quite thrilled her. Well, she immediately put on the girdle-cakes and wondered why they did not rise. But when she sampled them, it was she who rose, she nearly went mad for it was a strong bleaching soda. We are always obliged to ask what is this or that, it is all in small paper bags made up ready for us. We just grab the lot and are thankful for it. We have no palate left when we get real food. I just wonder how our tummies will react, at present mine is not too good. Thank goodness we live next to a farm and can get a pint of milk extra sometimes, butter is strictly rationed, but we get our share. It is really amazing how we are all bravely carrying on and making light of some of our biggest hardships. Every day I get wet feet (not too good at my time of life) but I come in, put my feet in hot water, change my stockings (sometimes footless) and, hi presto, different girl again. I have to go out, or I should go barmy, it's a thrill to get wet through.

November 8th, 1943

Poor Miss Hale has gone totally blind. She is being taken care of by Mrs C. Hamon. It is sad to see her lying so helpless when one remembers her being so energetic. She has been turned out of her house three times for military reasons. We are not out of the wood yet, anything may still happen. They have had some difficulty in getting tanks away, because since they landed them, the tunnel has been blocked up and wired (in case the English landed) so a great portion of the slipway and harbour had to be blasted, blast them!!! It will take hundreds of pounds to repair the Island and never will it be the same. There was some talk last week of blowing up the Coupée and the inhabitants being brought to big Sark, but I think it has boiled down to being heavily mined.

The German Army here at present are lads of about fifteen or sixteen, they just look like schoolboys.

Sunday, November 14th, 1943

A body has been washed up today in the Coupée Bay, one of our Marines, a stoker named Booth, poor fellow, I expect one of our boats has gone down quite near. Last week there were a lot of sinkings, planes overhead all day long, the big guns firing from Guernsey and sending shells whistling over Sark, some days it is quite alarming.

We have only three months' stores in advance in case there is a siege, but I would gladly give up some rations if it would hasten our release. Six sick men have been returned to their homes in Guernsey from Germany, but there is so little to eat over there. In Germany they said they would rather eat dry bread in their own homes than luxuries in the camp.

November 18th, 1943

It's very cold and wintry here today and there is quite a lot of illness about. Heavy colds, bronchitis, pneumonia, due mostly to the lack of nourishing foods. Sugar and fats we miss terribly. We don't get anything in our rations to make a pudding, or anything to tempt the appetite, and when we are feeling below par, it's a case of slow starvation. We all lack energy and feel we want to stay in bed, we do at least keep warm there. Norah is trying hard to carry on in school, but she is far from well, and all the children turn up like frozen rabbits, full of colds, and do nothing but cough and sneeze. The school would be better closed for the winter and the kids kept in bed. Please God this will be our last winter. We heard that Mr Churchill gave a speech in which he said, '1944 would be the worst year of the war, it would also be the last.'

A lot more of our Marines have been washed up in the bays in Guernsey. It's as well we cannot go into any of our beautiful little bays, I should think they are full of bodies, Germans and English. We only have the top of the Island to roam about in now, and half of that is wired off. We hear boxes and boxes of English toilet soap has been washed up but the Germans have collared it. We could do well with some of that, have a good wash and feel clean for once.

Why we buy the newspapers I don't know, for the Germans control all the news and only let us read what they want, or mean us to. 'Fuehrer's stirring speech, Germans to lay down arms only as victor'; 'Iron resolve of the German people'; 'If Germany lost, England would disappear'; 'Russia hopes to grasp Europe for herself'; 'Why Stalin hopes to turn England and America—red'; 'Germany out for victory, England for defeat.' Headlines such as these do not help to improve our drooping spirits, and some days we must be forgiven for being so down-hearted, the silver lining seems so far away.

I dreamt last night I was in Stockton market buying some lovely hard roe, bloaters and kippers, what I would not give for one for my tea this very minute and a good old English newspaper to read *our* news, no lies, lies, lies!

November 20th, 1943

I dreamt last night General Buller (of the Boer war) came to see me, his visit seemed a flying one, and all I can remember is he told me not to be down-hearted, in a hundred days something great was going to happen. I could not gather if it was our release from this awful prison life or a climax in the war, but he looked cheerful and happy, and it left me with a happy feeling. Of course everybody laughs at me for repeating it, and says, 'Do you believe in dreams?' Yes, I do and always have done! So I am going on, hopefully waiting for the end of February, that will be about the time, if then nothing has happened, well it has done me no harm and has helped to pass the weary hours. If we could only have a real letter from England for Christmas, a pair of shoes and stockings and 1lb of tea, it would give me new life.

157

November 29th, 1943

A German Officer for Agriculture came over last week and said the rats and rabbits must be poisoned. What will happen to our cats and dogs? It is wicked trying to keep any animals, they are underfed, like we are, and we cannot spare our food to feed them.

I had a nice surprise last week. The internees in Germany are allowed to send us a few cigarettes and Mr Phillips (our Vicar) sent me fifty. Thousands of cigarettes have come to the Island for the poor forsaken ones because they cannot afford the price of a smoke.

December 14th, 1943

I had to go to the German Commandant for a permit for wood today so as to be sure of a good fire for Christmas, if we get little else. Also I have had about half a dozen journeys and about as many papers to sign to get a pair of shoes from Guernsey. I must wait my turn which may be six months, and by then I shall be so used to wet feet every day I go out that I shall probably not mind going bare-foot, or the war may be over.

I am still trying to make rug-wool shoes for infants and small children, begging right and left for odd lengths and small balls, they are all rainbow colours, but who minds if they are warm. It would do you good to walk behind some of us and see the state of our heels and the remains of once good socks and stockings.

In Guernsey it is said they can get 25s a lb for butter. People are just dying for want of fat, some of the Sark farmers have been sending butter over there and reaping good prices, the Guernsey people don't mind what they pay for it. We are lucky to have new milk, they are only allowed skimmed milk there. Another old cow to be killed this week here, so perhaps a bit of suet will come our way. As regards the meat to eat we must 'Go to hell and stew.'

This week, our candle ration is to be reduced, to *one candle a week*. Imagine that! It gets dark soon after 5pm and we sew, patch or knit until 10pm then in the morning some light is needed to come downstairs, how far will one candle a week go?

It has turned very cold and frosty, we have also had a little snow. Really, bed is the best and warmest place. Thank God for that bit of comfort.

The bombing in France is terrific.

A big company went away yesterday and we had a little service in our church first. The poor men looked bored stiff with it, and none too pleased, who wants war? This lot don't look like soldiers at all and there is none of that mad running about the Island, mock battles, shooting everywhere and anywhere. The crack troops have all gone to Russia I suppose, the present lot look more like a lot of convicts, everywhere you see them with their picks and shovels, marching along with a young officer, looking more like a schoolboy, leading, what a farce it all is.

Mrs Hathaway sent me some rug-wool this week, and I am making some woollen shoes, she also sent some bits of leather to sole them with, these are for the schoolchildren to change into when they arrive in school with wet feet. We have had some torrential rains and the meadows have been flooded. Norah has broken up for the holidays. She says she would like to sleep through Christmas and the New Year. We have nothing to make Christmas cheer with this year, the fourth year of Occupation, but we have been invited to spend Christmas Day at a farm.

December 26th, 1943

It wasn't too bad yesterday (Christmas Day) and Norah and I went out all day long until 11pm, then we were sent home in a carriage in grand style. It was a glorious day just like September, and as we were returning I said it seemed too calm and peaceful to last, a sort of calm that gets on your nerves a bit. Mrs Hathaway sent me a 3lb packet of candles. Some unknown person in Guernsey sent me a large sack of wood. I had also some potatoes, turnips, carrots, onions, cabbage, leeks, cauliflower, some suet, a bottle of white wine, and our Vicar who is in Biberach sent me a slab of real English chocolate, also Miss Carter sent us a $\frac{1}{2}$lb block as well, they seem to get so much and it is kind of them to think of us poor neglected ones.

What did I say, 'it seemed too peaceful to last?' Well, what a night we had, it is a wonder our hearts did not stop. In the early hours of the night, about 2 or 3am, we were awakened by a thunderous knock on the door which kept on until we had the courage to leap out of bed, in the dark, and throw open the window to ask who was there. Four Germans stood there, fully armed and the officer said, 'Open the door at once'—they had come to search the house at that time of night. So we think some of the British have landed again and they think we may be harbouring them, what a nightmare, we had to follow them all over the house with hardly anything on, in bare feet. Two stayed by the front door fully armed on guard. The other two entered the house and began to search in the dining-room first, opening all cupboards, looking under sofas and tables, behind curtains, but the most amusing thing was my big black coat which was drying on a chair in front of the dining-room fire. They made straight for it, pointing their loaded revolvers in a very meaningful way, sure, it looked like a man crouching in front of the grate—remember, this was all being acted out by the light of a torch. I carried a small gleam. The procession went out of the dining-room into all those stone kitchens, Norah in her bare feet, everything turned topsy-turvy. Then they spied the back stairs. 'What's up here?' says the officer. 'You lead the way', so poor Norah had to go before them, you know what awkward stairs they are. If they had stumbled and the guns gone off, it was an awful thought. And the bedrooms are packed full of furniture, beds and curtains, mattresses and pillows piled on top of one another, blankets, all these were turned over and prodded with bayonets. Chests were opened, and everywhere left in an unholy mess and muddle. Then on to the front of the house, my bedroom first. Cupboards opened, beds searched under and over, wardrobes looked into, then Norah's bedroom and so on. Moth-proof dress-hangers opened and prodded and then when they got to the attic, Norah was again made to go before them, up those spiral stairs and I waited, it seemed hours altogether, and anything more degrading I have never known. We were perfectly in the dark as to why they were searching, and it was as much as our lives were worth to ask them. At last we got them out and locked the door, we crawled back into bed but could not sleep. We were thankful when dawn came and we could get some hot drinks, wish it could have been whisky!

December 27th, 1943

There has been another landing either at Dixcart or the Hog's Back and the search is still being carried on, we fear there will be another tightening up of rules. Two poor men, said to be French, are lying dead in a shed on a cold stone floor, they got to the land-mines. I don't know if they will be buried here or in Guernsey. I cannot see myself what good the landing down here does. The last one was October 1942 and brought us nothing but misery, especially to Mrs P. If it meant shortening the war we would not mind but all this is nerve-racking and I am afraid even my own shadow sometimes makes me jump.

December 30th, 1943

We were invited out to tea today to Miss Robinson's place, we met Mrs Hathaway and Mrs Skelton. The latter has quite recovered from her awful experience, but will she ever forget it?

I am so pleased the year is coming to an end, and pray to God the coming one will bring us victory and lasting peace everywhere. These last four years have been a big slice cut out of our lives, when we might have been of use to our country on the mainland.

I am making no plans for the New Year, I am leaving all to God. I remember last New Year's Day being so confident that it would be over in 1943. Now I feel a bit like Miss Robinson. If I ask her how long she thinks the war will last, she says, 'I have made up my mind it is going to last as long as I live, and if it is over before then I shall be pleased', and seeing she is only seventy-four and hale and hearty it's an awful thought.

January 2nd, 1944

I repeated on New Year's day the King's quotation of the first year of his Christmas message to his people.

'I said to the man who stood at the door of the year, give me a light that I may tread safely into the unknown and he replied, "go out into the darkness and put your hand into the hand of God. That shall be to you better than light and safer than a known way."'

Our Christmas was troubled by the landing of our men especially for us in the Dixcart Valley, but what an awful death for the two brave men. Some say they were French Canadians, the Germans called them gangsters and this reflects the treatment they received—Dennis Carre and his mate (who were both working for the Germans in Guernsey) overstayed their Christmas leave here, lost the boat through being drunk, so the German Commandant punished them by making them strip the two poor men who got on the mines and sew them in sacking, preparing them for burial—no military funeral for the two brave men who died for their country. The Seneschal was ordered to get two graves dug in our little churchyard and there they were thrown in at dawn one morning, not even a prayer said over them, poor dears. A wooden cross has been erected and their names put on and Mrs Hathaway sent two wreaths of camellia. Since then lots of little posies are constantly being put there, but it is all very sad. Two little bunches of flowers were tied with red, white and blue ribbon.

The Germans are very nervous and tense. They have now got six bloodhounds here and notices have been put up to say, 'Anyone found out after curfew will be treated as the enemy and punished accordingly.' We now know there were two landings of our men and we think they were here in the early evening and mixed with the people. I wonder. On one of the nights there was a Christmas dance on and the curfew was extended until 1am, what a wonderful bit of luck for them! A rumour says the BBC announcer reported that, 'The Sark landing was a great success.'

January 12th, 1944

Believe it or not, we have a bunch of roses on the table, a bunch of violets and primroses and some winter jasmine, also the bulbs are pushing up, and the gorse is out in bloom, so let's be cheerful!

The church was decorated again for Christmas, but we had no parson over from Guernsey, they all seem to be cracking up over there, the doctors as well. If anyone deserves the VC after the war it is the Guernsey doctors especially Dr Gibson, they are just worked to death, there is so much sickness. Sark patients are continually being sent over as well, and all mothers expecting babies are taken over for at least a month and some of the seas have been terrible for them to cross in, not counting the mines and other dangers to face. Those babies ought to have hearts of oak. I am sure the mothers have. Let us hope and pray they are not born to fight in another awful war.

A cutting out of our paper shows a photograph of an American airman who was shot down during a raid on Bremen. The Germans are getting very bitter and made fun of the crosses and prayer books found on the two dead men. They said they were armed with enough ammunition and guns to blow up the whole of Sark, but they dared to carry prayer books and crosses. They were only boys of about eighteen or so and what more natural than that their mothers would give them these with their blessings. I think they died bravely, alone on a dark cliff away from their mates. We hear since there were two landings that week, but so much goes on after curfew that they can cover up all tracks before it is light and the civilians are about again.

You probably know more about the doings of the little Island than we do. We hear from a friend that Sark is the envy of the Channel Islands. Mrs R. will never be able to go back to her home and they have now begun to pull down Robert's house. They are getting short of bricks so that is their method of getting some more. The cement and bricks are all taken up to the lighthouse end of the Island for they are making strong fortresses.

January 19th, 1944

I had a letter from Stephen H. in Guernsey the other day and in it he said, 'A lady in Guernsey had a Red Cross letter from her sister in England saying, "I am aching to be back home in Guernsey." The sister's reply was, "You will ache more when you do come back."' Things must be in a very bad state there, judging by the destruction going on over here.

I have had 2oz of real English Brooke Bond tea sent to me by our Vicar at Biberach, what a godsend it was, and almost sixteen people have had a cup of honest-to-goodness tea out of it to gladden our hearts. You bet how we thought and talked of you all, and the wonderful Red Cross. We hear now our Islanders will be able to send us a small parcel of things out of their Red Cross parcels. Will tell you what is in it later. God bless the Red Cross.

January 24th, 1944

There is an outbreak of chicken-pox on the Island and nearly all the children are away from school. Also many cases of appendicitis.

Last week was a really foggy one. One day the barge came in and it had on board a horse of Lanyon's that had cost £125 on Guernsey. The poor beast fell down in the horse box and had to remain in that position for hours. The boat could not put into the harbour until 7 in the evening, quite dark when they got the poor animal off but it had to remain on the jetty until the morning in the bitter cold, covered with coats and sacks. The two men remained with it and next morning got it to a warm stable but it died the next day.

This week it is blowing a heavy south-west gale and the sea is like a boiling-pot.

The Dixcart Valley is the centre of attraction now. They had a mock battle after the curfew the other night and even the blood-hounds took part. It is weird and horrible to hear them shuffling and parading around the house at night. Our dog growls and bristles all over but we dare not let him out. One dog has been nearly killed by them. The German troops are scared stiff and the likelihood of another landing means we don't dare be out after dark in case we are mistaken for the enemy!

I am going to see dear Mrs Toplis today for it's her birthday on Sunday and she will be eighty-six. We are beginning to barter and exchange rations etc, in that way we can get what we want for a time.

February 2nd, 1944

We are told our scanty newspaper will soon stop, no more paper. I shall not be sorry for the German news is appalling, they are always winning and England is as good as wiped out.

Here are some of Haw-Haw's headlines this week: 'Sacrifice to Stalin of Britain's sons butchered to make Bolshy'; 'Belts more tighter in England' (that is their grammar not mine); 'Britain falling between two stools, calm and complete confidence in Berlin.' I wonder!

We had a big saccharin ration this week, 400 each—twice as many as the last ration, also $\frac{1}{2}$gal of paraffin and two bags of coal, gosh! We feel quite rich all at once, it is the most we have had since the Occupation. We all wonder why but can only hope it is a good sign and things that have been in store are being released, and 'the silver lining is showing'. My dream about General Buller's 100 days is up about the end of this month. If that dream could only come true.

February 13th, 1944

A notice in the paper asks for all cars to be gathered up, they have shipped nearly all they could to Germany. Someone from Guernsey told me last week that he had seen eighty or a hundred beautiful grandfather clocks packed up ready for shipment and that they are mending boots in Guernsey with old rubber tyres. This week boots (working men's), if any can be had from France, are £2 and £3 a pair and working men's shirts 27s 6d each and the working man's wages only about 30s or 40s a week. I see some salted herrings are coming over and they are to be 1s 7d each, think of it! I remember in Liverpool when they sold forty for a shilling.

March 1st, 1944

It is bitterly cold, frosty, and we have had a heavy fall of snow. All the people in Little Sark have had to be evacuated over here and their cattle remain there, but it means them going backwards and forwards twice a day to tend them, jolly hard for them in frost and snow. There is an attack of influenza in Guernsey and a good many cases here. There is so little food to resist illness, the milk and butter shortage is acute, there is no food and very little grass for the cows, roots all gone. There are no potatoes and the bread rations are not enough for us.

Someone coming from Guernsey last week told me that some hundreds of cauliflowers were sent from the country parishes to a shop in town, and about fifty or sixty people queued up to buy them waiting in the cold, and then a German officer came along and bought them all up for the German troops. I believe they are slowly starving us to death. There is nothing to fatten pigs on and the hens won't lay without a bit of corn and the small farmer told me the other day that the German officers are riding right through the middle of his wheat field. It is quite common in Guernsey for people to attend an auction sale of cattle, buy one, kill it on the sly, and start a black-market selling. Eggs if you can buy them are about £5 a dozen, so how can the people live, they are dying off at a great rate.

Dear old Mrs Durand was buried last week, she was ninety-four. She was taken to Guernsey for they had a grave there. It is with the greatest difficulty a funeral can be carried out, there are practically no horses and no cars to be had, so it is a case of waiting your turn to be buried. Someone in Guernsey wants to bring in a death duty to help to balance the budget and one of the rectors said, 'we have to pay hard to live these days, without paying to die.' They are £2 million in debt and the troops are costing Sark £1,000 a year.

A notice in the paper warns, 'All concerned . . . that members of the German forces must be given priority attention in all shops and other establishments frequented by them. Severe punishment will be imposed on any who disregard this order.' This shows you how the heel has come down, we get so weary waiting day after day for news that never comes.

March 6th, 1944

Hurrah!! We hear the parcels from Biberach have arrived in Guernsey and we eagerly expect them in Sark. The joy and thrill of having something direct from England. It seems really amazing it can only be about eighty miles away and we have been cut off for four years, what we shall have to tell each other and I hope it is not far off now.

There are just as many troops here as ever, just young boys, getting drilled every minute of the day, some of them don't look more than fifteen or sixteen. Destruction goes on just the same every day, houses pulled down, and wood and stone taken away to make more dug-outs and fortresses.

It is now possible for *them* to get from the lighthouse (all underground tunnel) to the harbour, over Robert's Common through La Valette grounds. The weather is a bit better, still very cold, but dry and sunny. I saw a film once where the hero and the heroine were stranded in some out of the way place and they were sitting chewing turnips out of a field nearby. I can remember thinking, 'what rot', and I never imagined it was possible, but turnips are our mainstay stable diet and my views are changed.

Someone has given me a few handfuls of broad beans and a few early seed potatoes, and I am putting them in the garden trusting to luck and that the rats and rabbits will leave them alone, but I doubt it, we are overrun with vermin, troops included. The only things that are really happy are the birds, they sing all day long from early in the morning and no one feeds them, so that should give us hope and more heart.

March 9th, 1944

Cheers! and a grateful thank you to the Red Cross and our friends in Biberach. The parcels turned up today and what happiness and excitement there is in Sark. I feel like a real 'Bob Cratchett'. It gave me most pleasure when sharing my titbits with other needy ones, I saw poor little Pattie's face, because although she could not see the packet she fingered, one could see she was revelling in it. Contained in the parcels were real tea, honest-to-goodness cocoa, Rowntrees, margarine, oats, syrup, sugar, cheese, eggs, flakes, cigarettes, tobacco, chocolate and soap. A real glad week for us I can tell you. German news would have us believe that Britain is starving, how can we believe it when such parcels are sent from the Red Cross? Surely Sark is the only place in the world at the present time where the Red Cross does not operate, for our parcels can only be sent through our friends, who have gone to Biberach. We heard yesterday from a visitor from Guernsey that it was announced by the BBC thirteen prisoners were taken away from Sark a week or two ago, how little we know or are allowed to know. We are told there are a few wireless sets hidden somewhere and the penalty is well worth it.

March 18th, 1944

A sad accident happened last week in the Dixcart Valley. Mr John Carre was engaged in cutting down a tree at Dixcart when the tree unexpectedly gave way, crashed down and caught Mr Carre, pinning him so gravely that his back was broken. He expired fifteen minutes later. Poor Bertha (his sister) will take years to recover from the shock.

Clothes too are now becoming unobtainable. Curtains, blankets, any old rags are being asked for to make vests and pants or any useful garment. The invasion is still talked of and expected, and rumour went round that it would be the 16th of this month. Two days have passed since then and all is quiet. The poor old windmill, a landmark on the Admiralty chart, is being demolished, or partly, I think they are putting guns or a strong searchlight on top for they are always expecting another landing in the Dixcart Valley.

Our curfew is 10pm and it is light now until about 8.30pm. A notice up this week by the German Commandant, 'All civilians found out after curfew will be shot', how nice! I think I would rather be shot than mauled by the wretched dogs, bloodhounds or Alsatians. We hear them barking at night.

March 28th, 1944

Yesterday, Sunday, the bombing and noise fairly shook the house to the foundations. We are told it was at Cherbourg, it appears to us to be the whole of France, it is night and day bombing, and never leaves off. Last night after curfew planes were going over the island by the hundred, it was an incessant noise all night long. Some seem to stand still or encircle the island. The dear old mill looks like a fierce wild animal by day, what it looks like at night goodness only knows, but by day it is covered with heavy tarpaulins to hide search-lights and guns—everywhere one looks there are hideous signs of war and death traps.

Another sad thing has happened on our little Isle. Jacqueline Carre fell jumping over a high bank one night and broke her leg. She was attended by the German doctor, kept in the German Red Cross hospital here all night, then in the morning taken to our hospital in Guernsey. Since then we hear she has had her leg off above the knee. You know what a fine healthy girl she was, only nineteen, her parents are distracted, she is the only child, they are with her in Guernsey. It is amazing how the doctors carry on in the face of great shortages of everything, particularly nourishing food, helping the sick to recover. A paragraph in the paper from one of the dentists' wives whose husband has been very ill, thanks all those who, as a result of a notice she put in the paper for any bits of nourishing food to be sent to her, has now recovered. Another notice in the press says that candles have come to an end, God, what shall we do? It is amazing to see also that salt-water can be bought by the gallon as there is practically no salt. For some time people have been boiling vegetables in sea-water, everything is very tasteless. We hear now that about 800 German planes circled round and round the four Islands incessantly on Sunday, and they were on their way to England and that Bristol has been heavily bombed.

I keep wondering if you are still in your home, or if that side of the coast has been evacuated, no message from you for months now. I keep looking at the babies' photos and wonder how old they will really be when I do see them, if ever.

A message from a lady friend in Germany says, 'We are trying to keep a tight clutch on our sanity.' Forgive me for being dismal, dear, but as the days and months pass I begin to lose heart, sometimes. Judith will be four in July and I expect talks about her Granny and Auntie Norah. I have sent a birthday wish for Judith in July, through Germany.

Easter Sunday, April 9th, 1944

Once again Easter Day has come around and here we are penned up still, it really seems impossible, four years of it. The little church was decorated once again by willing workers, and looked beautiful. No person could come from Guernsey for the services, one will come next week. Nearly all the clergy are ill in Guernsey and there are so few left to take services.

Things are daily getting worse in the food line, it is almost famine now and people are looking old and gaunt. Here in Sark we have no fresh meat, not even tinned to take its place, no fish (the fishermen are not allowed out because of the mines etc.), no potatoes, no vegetables, no flour and insufficient bread. So how can we last much longer?

Easter Monday, April 10th, 1944

By a German command a football match was played by Sark boys and Germans, the Germans won 7–0. In the evening a dance had been arranged by the Sark young folk. The Germans all turned up at the hall, the German doctor and the Commandant included, but when they arrived they were drunk and at the end of it had to be carried off to Headquarters by the soldiers. They allowed the Sark boys to go to the canteen for as much brandy as they liked and by the end of the evening some of the Sark men were 'Heiling Hitler' and rolling home drunk. In all the countries they have taken over I don't think they could have possibly had such excellent material to mould to their liking, it is too disgusting for words. What an excellent time it would have been for a landing in Sark while they were all rolling drunk.

April 17th, 1944

The news has come from Guernsey today that Jacqueline passed away after another operation this morning, it has cast a whole gloom over the island. Her parents and grandparents are distracted, there seems to be nothing but sadness and funerals lately.

April 20th, 1944

Poor Jacqueline was brought over from Guernsey today and buried in the little churchyard. Everyone in Sark attended the funeral and there were about 150 wreaths of lovely flowers, it is a ghastly accident to have ended so fatally. The first amputation was above the knee, then gangrene set in more quickly and it was amputated to the hip, the dear girl died soon after.

April 22nd, 1944

A peaceful Sunday, not a sound anywhere. On Hitler's birthday I had a bit of a fright. On my way to the village I spied a huge flag with a swastika on, flying on top of the old mill, and my first thoughts were, 'have the Germans conquered?' My heart stood still until I remembered it was Hitler's birthday.

I am so weary of this Occupation and the sight of the Germans and the daily waiting for some good news. Another shell has fallen and buried itself on Robert's Common. The devils are still digging themselves in.

It is said they are going to build a cinema near the mill and thousands of bricks are being sent over for the purpose.

April 26th, 1944

Many happy returns dear Norah and I hope your next birthday will be spent in England and all the hardships forgotten like a bad dream.

There is a terrible noise of planes and guns and bombs and shells bursting over the Island, one wonders if there will be any France left. The German troops cannot go on leave, the ports are blocked, so reports say what food we do get may stop next week. We heard that the invasion has started somewhere but we don't know where and that we have landed in Cherbourg. I wonder.

May 1st, 1944

Here we are into our fifth month and still no hopeful signs of seeing you, but cherry blossom time is here again and perhaps the prophecy may be meant to work out this year. If we could be heartened the birds are giving every sign of victory, they sing loudly from morn till eve and even through misty moonlight nights their little throats are bursting. The cuckoo is really too noisy.

I had a pathetic letter from Miss Carter in Germany this week, she says that they have all been ill. The eighteen in her room and in fact all the camp came through a very hard cold winter, snow and frost never leaving off except to freeze harder at nights, everyone down with flu and everyone coughing all night long. Just try to realize it and she has had a lot blocked out of her letter but by a little cleverness Norah reads, 'there are no remedies or drugs of any kind to give relief', they evidently don't like us to know that part of life in prison camp. She also says they never see a flower and they had no walk for months because of the snow. She did love her cottage in Sark and the wild flowers, she was a real nature lover.

We have been having a spring clean, had our old Philip, he is splendid, but all of it was carried out without soap, there is not a bit on the Island. How we keep going is marvellous, it must be the rainwater we use that helps to cleanse. I hope there will be some soap in the Red Cross parcels if they ever arrive.

The crime wave still goes on here and in Guernsey. Two Sark boys were sent over to Guernsey for trial last week, they stole six or seven hens from the postmistress. They really ought to have been imprisoned, a bad pair, but we have since heard the prison in Guernsey is full and will hold no more, and the Sark prison is part of the German Headquarters so it's all a happy hunting ground.

May 17th, 1944

There seems another of those silences over the little Island again. No one is to leave the Island or come over from Guernsey and all leave is stopped for the present. I tremble as I write at the thought of how I will react when any real happening occurs. I manage, except on very rare occasions, to keep myself in bounds and try to find the bright spots. I go out as much as possible and thank God for the sunshine and flowers and letting me stay in my home so far.

There is great restlessness among the German troops, they say themselves they wish the English would come, and the war would end. Planes (ours) have been flying very low and lots of this ribbon paper fluttering down on the Island. We wonder what it is thrown down for. Norah says it is to do with photos they are taking over the Islands, others say it is to stop any news being put over (morse), so I will keep ribbons and perhaps have it explained. A newspaper report contains some bitter words about poor old Winston, our news is getting very bitter but thank God he keeps his health to direct the nation, he surely has a heart of oak without drinking acorn coffee.

A lot of German high officials have been over again re-laying more mines. They seem terrified of another landing here and are daily expecting an invasion. When the German officers returned to the harbour they were seated in arm chairs on a huge motor lorry, wobbling about down the harbour hill, it is a great pity our cameras were taken away and we often see the reason why. How I envy you with wirelesses, the daily news up to date of all the world affairs and no German lies to poison your minds, it is a great wonder we keep sane.

Some of these troops here now have been in Russia for two years. The man who has charge of this powerhouse at the mill is a Cypriot, and it is he who doles out little drops of paraffin as we are allowed. He, it is said has a bet on of £50 or £100 that by the 16th June this year, we shall have paraffin from England and be in communication. Oh, if it is only true, in less than a month's time!

Last night I dreamt I was in one of Lyon's tea shops eating wonderful spice cakes in great hunks and I saw piles of luscious red strawberries. Sure, food gets scarcer than ever, we are told all the French ports are closed, so boats get fewer. Our rations this week, little bit of salt, a bit of coffee, and about $\frac{3}{4}$lb of flour, it's surely starvation diet for the bread is not enough, and out of it we have to feed the dog and five hens.

There was a mock invasion battle last week all night long but we did not know until the next day it was a mock battle. It was a hellish night, no sleep for anyone, guns going off, mines exploding at every point on the cliff. A number of huge mines were placed at different points all round the cliff and, at a given signal hurled to the bottom, the noise was like hell let loose. As we lay shivering and heard the mines going off we only thought it was some of our men landing and getting on the mines. They have a huge ship's bell outside Headquarters marked 'Gas Alarm', then that began to ring violently, so altogether it was a hectic night.

June 1st, 1944

We have spent another Whitsuntide and the little church has been decorated once again by the faithful few. Our Vicar wrote from Biberach and said how happy it made them all to feel there that the services went on in his absence, the Rev Guille came over for Trinity Sunday, and took services.

A Spitfire came down in the Russel one day but we don't know how many were saved, we were told by someone who saw it happen. A plane then came from England and dropped a boat from a parachute to find our men in the water near the wreck but the man or men were so injured they were taken prisoners to Guernsey and some of our men came back and bombed the boat that sank them.

Our boys have made two or three attacks on Fort George in Guernsey, and in the one on Whit Monday (at a German football match) they say 180 were killed and a lot of houses wrecked. We seem intent on getting the devils out this time, the attacks are so determined and awful while they last. The planes were all overhead, it looks like a real siege, but we are bracing ourselves up for any emergency if it only means getting them out, the Germans have thoroughly got the wind up now for they can see they are trapped like rats which they are.

June 7th, 1944

We hear today we have got Rome and landed in France in five places. It is strange how the news does trickle through, we can only suppose it comes through the Germans and almost all of them say, 'they wish the English would land and end all their misery', they look quite fed up and short of food like us. The Guernsey guns do not seem so frequent or so noisy. I think our boys have found them and put them out of action, why the devils do not give in and clear off I don't know. They must know their number is up. Lots of German boats are in the Guernsey harbour, I suppose waiting to take them away but I am afraid they have left it too long.

They have slung huge mines everywhere round the cliffs of Sark, at the Coupée they are cemented to the brickwork and structure underneath the path itself, and we believe if they have time before leaving they will blow it up or, if our boys land at Little Sark, shut them off from getting further. We are all agog with excitement and we don't know what we shall wake up to any morning now. Cheers!

June 8th, 1944

There is an English destroyer in Guernsey Harbour, the news thrills us both so that we can hardly eat any supper (bread and pullet). We hear now that there is no destroyer in Guernsey Harbour. The drought has become serious, we have had no rain since February, all crops are suffering, and we are short of water. Since the invasion began the Germans have barricaded themselves into their quarters. The jolly little Slovak who I told you was crying a week ago because the English would not be quick in coming (he is a bright happy boy about fifteen or sixteen) is the only bright spot in this German lot. All he wants to do is to get home to his mother. I wonder if he will be taken prisoner. We are cut off from everywhere, no mail, no rations. The curfew is to be earlier and lots more things tightened up. How we ache to hear a bit of good true news. After all the anxious months of dark days and terror.

June 10th, 1944

The Rev Guille who came to take our services last week met with an accident and hurt his leg and by special command a boat was chartered to take him to Guernsey, also the appendix case and a case of scarlet fever and diphtheria, so a real hospital ship left the little harbour to brave the terrors of this awful bit of sea from here to Guernsey. We cannot hear how they are going on, no phone, no nothing.

We hear great rumours of things that are about to happen on the waters all around this week, and all boats and shipping are to cease running. We are promised our rations once a week, but as they are so meagre and few it won't hurt us to go without for a week or two, if it is helping the cause. We all feel so glad and excited. I feel it in my bones that we are going to be released soon. A good bit of damage has been done in Guernsey but it is unavoidable as the German big guns are scattered all over the Island, even erected on the tops of civilians' houses.

Although it seems they must be on the eve of leaving the Islands (lots of the heads have left Guernsey already), goodness knows if they will ever reach France. The bombing and fighting on the sea is terrific, day and night, but even now they are digging themselves further in and more huge mines are being put almost up to our very doors. There is even one in the churchyard. Wooden sign-boards are erected nearby with grinning skulls and crossbones on, and the targets they shoot at when practising appear to be photos of poor old Winston, what a pleasure it must give them.

June 12th, 1944

The Commandant here says he will fight to the last man, they have had orders from Hitler to fight to the last man and not be taken prisoner if it can be helped, because if they do so only concentration camp in Russia awaits them and they will never see the Fatherland again. There are only about 200 troops here now and as most of them are foreigners, Poles, French, Slovaks etc., their hearts are not in the fight. In Guernsey there is more panic now than when the Germans landed four years ago. In Jersey I think it is just as bad, the raids are very heavy and very sudden, hardly any warning and no time to take cover. Here in Sark, although the whole Island is burrowed and tunnelled, we have no shelter to go to. If half the mines they have laid go off, this little Island will go up in smoke.

Our boys come daily and bomb and machine-gun, nearly always getting their objective, but I wish they would pop the Headquarters, the Manoir, and the guns on the mill, for if they got the heads the poor men would gladly give in. This seems as if it will be a critical week in our history, and I mentioned to you previously that the Cypriot told me two or three months ago to go home and mark my calendar the 16th June, that's Friday, so we hope for great things. I dreamt of fish last night, hundred of bloaters, hard roes and soft. I went to see Miss Mac. yesterday, she is over the moon with joy and thrilled to think we are soon going to be free, she is starting to pack for good old Scotland.

June 15th, 1944

Another hellish night, but we know our boys are quite close to us and anything might happen quite suddenly. Yesterday at midnight more German anti-aircraft were sent over and are being erected all over the Island. Their boat leaves at midnight from Guernsey with food, guns, ammunition etc ... Every boat is accompanied by two or three gunboats flying the swastika. If they would let the *White Heather* come along flying the Guernsey flag I know none of our planes would bomb or machine-gun it. More fields and plots are taken off the farmers for mines and gun emplacements, whole crops of wheat and potatoes are being dug up everywhere by German command before they are ripe, and they are only given a few hours to clear out the unripe wheat which is fed to cattle. So much land has been taken from the farmers, grassland especially, that the poor beasts are nearly starving and the drought of nearly three months is very serious indeed, no rain since February except a few slight showers.

The little Slovak says when the English come he will strip his green uniform off, stamp on it and welcome the English forces in his shirt alone. The funniest side and sights of this fight, I feel, are still to come. Jolinette says (he fought in the last war), 'I will help the English when they come and glory in it.' He is one, and there are only a few, who have not worked for the Germans. Most of the Island men are working for them and helping to carry these treacherous mines to catch our boys when they do come. I pray to God that is not how we shall be freed.

Sunday, June 18th, 1944

There have been German destroyers in Guernsey Harbour today but we are told that they have been bombed by our planes and set on fire. The noise of deafening bombing from Guernsey, Jersey, Alderney and France is constant. Mines and guns are placed around the church, boys' school, the hall and churchyard. We are told a wire is attached to all and if the Germans go in a hurry they can all be let off to blow their quarters up, but unfortunately some of our quarters too, also great iron stakes or girders are being erected in almost every field, explosives on top of them to prevent parachutes or planes landing there, the whole Island is a death trap to everybody.

Today we are feeling very sad, Norah and I. The Germans have shot our little dog, he was such a lovable little chap and so faithful to us both. They say he got on a minefield behind Vieux Clos and if they had not shot him it would have been danger for us. I don't believe them, they are a bloodthirsty race and love to kill, our turn may come next, who knows? Norah has been three times to Head-quarters to see if we could have the body to bury him but they even

175

refuse us that, we would have liked to have buried him under the beech tree at the Dixcart Hotel as his mistress is away in the German camp.

Another date has gone by, the 16th June, and nothing has happened yet, the firing of guns and bombs is terrific night and day. We heard a rumour yesterday that we had got to Cartaret, our nearest bit of France, so no wonder we hear the noises so much. The German newspapers still declare they are winning all the time.

June 21st, 1944

When Fort George (in Guernsey) was raided a short time ago, the German radio station was knocked to pieces so the Germans here are quite isolated, they can get no news at all through, and rumour says the cables are all cut to France so all communications are cut off. A little news leaks out for there are still one or two wirelesses in Guernsey although a number of people are in gaol for spreading news. Lanyon, the baker, has got six months and the prisons are so full they have to take their turn to go until some have finished their sentences. When the invasion started on June 6th some hundreds of people in Guernsey went nearly mad with joy and excitement singing, 'Roll out the Barrel', and 'There'll always be an England', and lots of the German soldiers joined in. For punishment, two or three hours have been taken off the curfew, all cinemas, concert halls and places of amusement are closed until further notice, the schools are also closed but not the churches. Lots of people were hurt by flying shrapnel when the raids were on.

We talked last night about the fashions in London and wondered how long the skirts were worn and if feathers and flowers were put in hats. The fashions in Sark at the present time would beat any place in the world.

June 22nd, 1944

Things are hotting up. All day long the guns have been thundering away and thousands of planes flying overhead, we feel it must be Alderney and Cherbourg they are taking, but we have no means of knowing except by the direction of sound.

The Germans here only get themselves more mined in, there are not many inches in Sark that are not mined so that it is hardly safe to walk about, also they must be getting very short of food, no boat from France for three or four weeks. I hope they won't take our little bit of food. One Sark man has had his cows milked early in the morning by the soldiers and they are going round from house to house making plans to buy hens or potatoes, we were told not to feed the enemy but Sark people are selling them all they want.

June 29th, 1944

We had a boat from Guernsey yesterday, we know definitely that Cherbourg is taken though not Alderney but five or six boatloads of Germans and civilians (labour gang) have been taken off Alderney and very few soldiers remain. Talk says the guns have been put out of action. The conditions in Guernsey are appalling. Food, water, gas and electricity shortages are very serious indeed. We have had rain at last, all the wells are dried up, so we can do with a lot more.

It is four years today since the Occupation and I thought something was going to be saved for this day but perhaps we shall not be relieved until more of the coast of France is taken. I pray and trust there will be no fighting, for the Island folks have suffered quite enough.

July 1st, 1944

We thought something would happen on 28th June since Cherbourg was taken but we all hope it is our turn next. The poor folk in Guernsey had a terrible time last week, a bomb was dropped on the harbour and there was a terrible amount of damage. The whole of the High Street, Mill Street, Bordage and Esplanade. Not any lives lost fortunately but a few people were hurt and cut by flying glass, there are hardly any windows left. German submarines were in the harbour and we hear today that our Navy is only about twelve or fourteen miles away. So anything may happen this week. The people have been issued with two weeks' rations and told to stop in their houses, so it looks as if they really mean it this time. Our little boat was allowed to come on Saturday with our few rations and mail with no gunboat escort at all, not even German guards on board, so the Germans *must* be scared stiff to put out to sea. It's laughable, even now our Sark fishermen are ordered to go out to sea and fish this week, and if they don't obey it will be taken as an act of sabotage. We want the fish very badly but not at the cost of men's lives. Bob Hurley is home from Alderney after the awful raid there last week. 2,000 civilians and 1,000 political prisoners have been taken off the Island after being given half an hour's notice to quit. Only two old couples refused to leave, so they remain. He says that the Americans drop bombs that cut right through solid cement walls six or nine feet thick, just as if it were paper.

July 4th, 1944

We cannot tell what is happening it is all so very quiet, not a sound of a gun anywhere, only the sound of the Germans blasting rocks around the coast. Although we appear to be on the eve of relief there is more destruction than ever going on. More houses are pulled down to reinforce their tunnel dug-outs. I have been drying rose petals today to vary the drinks, I am told it makes good tea, what our insides will be like, I don't know, with all the concoctions we put into them. The men are also drying them to eke out the tobacco ration.

The lovely old town church in Guernsey has had all its stained glass windows blown out except two panes, it is such a shame on the eve of relief.

The weather is good, the garden produce is a great help and luxury, also we get a few tomatoes from Guernsey which help the awful bread down. The garden is a great relief and joy, and the roses and every flower give us hope and pleasure of happier days to come. I have given up trying to realize or picture the joy it will give me to see you all and the mainland again, for so many of my dreams have gone awry. I try to keep busy, I make no plans, just trust in God and wait his time. Poor Miss Mac. has already packed up and is awaiting the first plane to England. I shall be glad to see her off for she needs a lot of care and her sister's assistance.

July 10th, 1944

There has been a terrible battle going on in France, seems like Granville and St Malo. The Germans here are erecting huge iron pipes six or eight feet high all over the pastures and fields of corn to prevent planes and parachutes from landing, and on the tops of them are explosives. They have started again to blast the tunnel in Stock's Meadow to link it up with the Headquarters at the Manoir. The food problem still grows, there has been no meat in Guernsey this week or for four weeks, but horses were killed this week and the meat served out. There is talk that the Germans will take all the cattle if there is a siege here on Sark, all the calves are being killed off at six weeks old. There are no pigs anywhere.

The noise of guns and bombing has stopped and it is quiet, but for how long? The fishermen have been forced to go out under penalty of death to get fish, even though small boats were told to keep off the seas at the present time, fact is, the Germans are nearly starving and they collar the fish. We get what they don't want, and wait their pleasure every time.

July 18th, 1944

I don't think I can stand more of it and Norah is a bundle of nerves. We know nothing and hear less, no news of what *we* are doing, whether we are winning or losing. We did not realize when we had the wirelesses how well off we were. I once thought if it was ever taken away from us I should go mad. Strange what we have had to get used to, all of us were given receipts for them when they were handed in and told that we should have them back one day, but now they are probably all smashed up somewhere like the guns and cameras.

There was a terrific noise last night, it sounded as if it might be Granville. We have given up hoping for deliverance until the whole coast is taken as far as Brest and there is no sign of the devils leaving this Isle. Their food must be very short by now, you would think that would shift them, but no, they are starting to pinch ours. As I told you they will take the Island cattle, it is true some of the cows look very lean and miserable and it *has* been a great struggle to keep them alive, but some of them are so valuable and after the war will be even more so. It will be sad to see them slaughtered for food.

July 20th, 1944

Things seem to be warming up in Jersey and beyond, there is incessant firing and gun-fire. Two of *our* own warships were off the Sark coast yesterday. The lighthouse guns opened fire, but no answer from ours, for which we are glad as one blast would probably put the Island off the map. The newspaper depresses us, it says, 'we are losing in France and being driven back everywhere.' I remember thinking at the end of two years that we could bear no more, so how we have ever stuck it this far I don't know. It has just been existing not living.

On Sunday night a lot of the troops got drunk and started fighting. It was a political fight and there was shooting going on, we could hear it until the early hours of the morning. It must have been the Nazis and the Slovaks and the Poles. Several men have been taken to hospital in Guernsey badly wounded, so it looks a good sign for us if they are fighting amongst themselves.

July 22nd, 1944

Jersey Airport has been bombed today and two German ships sunk in Guernsey Harbour fully loaded with guns and ammunition, also men.

July 24th, 1944

We hear Hitler has been shot but he is still alive, worse luck. I hope the next time will be his lucky time. We also hear (it may be only a rumour) that the Russians are only ten miles off the frontier. There has been another row and fight amongst the troops here. There is also great unrest in Guernsey. When the *White Heather* comes over with our rations we get wee bits of news by the crew and they take bits of Sark news back to Guernsey.

Our rations this week for two only came to 1s 6d, so if it were not for our few potatoes and vegetables from the garden it would be starvation diet.

The *White Heather* flies the white flag and comes unescorted now, but this week when she was almost ready to leave Guernsey the Germans loaded her up with mines, ammunition and all kinds of explosives for Sark until she was heavy and quite low in the water. They are asking for blood-donors in Guernsey, it will be terrible if they fight in the Islands. Another rumour is that leaflets have been dropped telling civilians to keep away from gun emplacements.

I am weary of waiting for my good cup of tea, coffee or cocoa, something to act as a stimulant to buck me up a bit, after three weeks of feeling weak and weary I am at last getting rid of my bruises and aches and pains. I don't bounce like I used to.

August 1st, 1944

Two nights ago a boat came from Guernsey at midnight full of explosives and a huge gun. The tunnel from Stock's to the Manoir is being fitted with mattresses taken from houses, so I suppose it is to be a nice cosy dug-out for the officers to run to in case our boys do land. The fishermen in Guernsey have absolutely refused to go out, but in Sark they are forced to under penalty of death. A great need at the present is for a bit of soap or soon some of us will have a skin disease. Also as the days begin to draw in we need candles or paraffin and matches but none are to be got, heaven help us if many more weeks go by. What the Germans are trying to hold on to these Islands for, I don't know, they must be a big expense to them and the loss of boats and men are appalling.

Norah's revelling in her holidays, living in the garden, the weather is not too bad, but not exactly summery. There are a lot of gay flowers out to gladden our hearts and a good promise of apples and blackberries, if we could only get a ration of sugar for jam. We eagerly await a Red Cross ship and a cup of good tea.

August 3rd, 1944

A friend sent us over a basket of tomatoes from Guernsey today, and in the centre a big water melon, such a treat and a surprise, then I went to visit a friend and she gave me a big lobster, already boiled. Five minutes after this Mrs F. came in with a big dish of raspberries with some cream on, three big lettuces with nice white hearts and a boiling of French beans. Gosh, it looked like a birthday party and pre-war days!

There is awful gun fire and explosions today near Jersey and an attack in Guernsey Harbour. There is a German boat already loaded there which has been waiting for days to get away but chances are few now as all ports are closed up.

August 6th, 1944

The Germans had an alarm at about 7pm tonight and they instantly sent for all carts and horses on the Island to take their entire goods and chattels down to the harbour, the poor men and horses were carting until 5am as fast as they could. All livestock except horses, pigs, goats, rabbits and hens, guns and ammunition, in fact, it seemed like a real clear out, so much so, that I immediately went up to the attic and unearthed a Union Jack, I want to be the first to get back to pre-war days and a purer atmosphere. The whole place here is poisonous, the air, the people, mostly the Islanders, they have no time for the English because they have all gone German-mad, and not one of them has done a thing for the country. Six boats came over from Guernsey last night with another company. It seems strange as our planes have not been over for days that these troop-ships can be allowed to come and go safely.

181

We hear a rumour this week that our boys have landed in Jersey, that we have got St Malo and Granville and that it is a complete cut-off for the Germans, also that Jersey has been given an ultimatum, so we feel the day of rejoicing has nearly arrived.

August 12th, 1944

Alas, here we are still, like birds in the wilderness. There has been a terrible battle in the Channel all night long, the whole valley rattled with the sound of the naval guns but when the morning comes we hear all sorts of rumours, never the truth. I expect it was some of the German boats trying to get away, but where to? The men are quite resigned to giving themselves up but the officers, not so, every port seems closed to them now and food is very short indeed for all of us.

August 19th, 1944

A large convoy tried to leave Guernsey today under cover of fog but was attacked by our warships half-way there. An awful battle went on although it was too misty to see it and several boats were lost, the sea must be full of dead bodies. There are too many troops to feed in Guernsey and as the State of Germany cannot feed their own people the Germans are trying to even them out and send hundreds to Jersey. I don't know if there is much more food in Jersey, seems to me we shall be starved out soon. When Alderney was so badly bombed by us three weeks ago all the civilians were sent to Guernsey, so there are many hundreds more to provide for. The bread ration is cut down again this week.

Lanyon, our baker, came out of prison this week, he looked very thin and careworn. He says he had the first solitary confinement, he got six months for trying to cheer us all up by telling us bits of news. Now another chap has been caught (but he has escaped), the charge says theft but he was in possession as well of a transmitter and a wireless, he is still hiding, meanwhile all his relations and dependants are being punished.

I saw two soldiers on Sunday sitting down eating a billy-can full of blackberries, they said they are our prisoners now as the Channel Islands are cut off. I would like to know whose prisoners any of us are. All the transmitter men were sent off the Island this week, not wanted here, because all communications with France are cut off.

August 26th, 1944

I dreamt last last night I was at a party eating food of all sorts. We went to Little Sark the other day to see the heather on the cliffs (the only part not mined). We took our tea and sat in deep heather gazing out to sea, but the destruction at the Vermandaye and the bungalow hotel cannot be described. Every article of furniture smashed up as if an axe had been used on it, books torn up, valuable volumes burnt in the fire grate. Last night I went for a walk to Clos de Dixcart and that is worse, the whole structure of the house is ruined, central beams taken away and all the linings gone, now they have started on the outside of it. It was a sad sight at Petit Dixcart, at Ponpattie house also. How my heart aches for the poor people who may come back to see their homes smashed up. The officers' horses are half starved, they have let them loose in the churchyard and they wander amongst the gravestones eating the flowers on the graves and kicking over the glass globes. The troops are hungry too, they go from house to house asking for milk and eggs, potatoes or apples.

We hear that Paris is taken and good headway is being made in France. Two beautiful horses left Sark today for Guernsey to be killed for meat.

For some time now lots of advertisements have appeared in the paper about dogs and cats being lost and heads and whole skins of the lost ones are being found, proving that they are being used for food. Talk says it is the foreign workers who are nearly starving. A Guernsey man was shot in the tummy this week and his son was injured by a German because they had been having their crop of potatoes stolen. The father and son had sat up to watch for the thief. Here in Sark they are stealing the potatoes also. Two soldiers were sent over from Guernsey this week to buy up eggs, butter or chickens to take back for the officers in Guernsey.

September 3rd, 1944

This is the anniversary of the war breaking out five years ago today. It would seem the devils are still digging themselves more firmly in. We hear a hundred more Marines are to come to Little Sark, what they will eat I don't know. We are told there is only enough food for a fortnight for us civilians. There has been a special meeting in Guernsey and one of the doctors suggests it is either the white flag or starvation and all sorts of lights are being asked for urgently to supply the hospitals, gas and electricity have given out. We also hear that leaflets have been dropped asking the German troops to give up and avoid bloodshed.

Norah has gone back to school today after five weeks' holiday, the day she broke up she was jubilant. She said, 'Surely in five weeks something will have happened', and here we are like a lot of cabbages. Our brains are dull, there seems nothing to look forward to. Some folk have already started to write letters to England ready for *the day* but I will wait until the white flag is really hoisted.

Three weeks ago I got my Union Jack out, that was one of my bright days, yesterday I put it away again for it seems awful to see more guns and tons of ammunition being carted to Little Sark this week, and the soldiers are stripping the hotels and houses once again for beds, mattresses, furniture and all sorts, and so it goes on.

September 5th, 1944

Hush! Not a word. I have seen some English wireless news, which says, 'we are in Germany and the war may end in a fortnight.' Gosh! It nearly takes my breath away. I cannot take it in. Our brains refuse to take it in, to think that we shall get a real English newspaper, perhaps our wirelesses back, and return to a happier and saner world. We can bear being prisoners for a fortnight although there is no sign of a white flag being hoisted.

Sunday, September 10th, 1944

I always like to put the year, in case we go into two or three more.

It is a glorious sunshiny day, real summer weather and the only sounds are the troops practising shooting because they are all preparing to fight. Hitler says they must fight to the last man and their names will go down in history. The rebels won't give up! It will be awful if, after struggling for four years to keep alive, we are bombed out, for I cannot see what else we can do, only bomb them out, blast them, for bringing all this misery on the whole world. If they do start to fight for the Islands we have nowhere to run for safety, no dugouts or trenches to creep to.

Last night I dreamt I had found a 7lb biscuit tin in the garden full of all good things. Yesterday more news came from Guernsey that brandy, cigarettes and tobacco had been dropped in Guernsey. Leaflets have been dropped in Sark, but nothing else.

September 15th, 1944

Well here we are, a fortnight is up and still no sign of the Germans leaving us. But we hear Brest is still being fought for. We wonder if it is true. Sometimes I think will we ever believe anything we hear again after this, so many lies have we had to swallow during this Occupation. I find myself saying when given any news, 'is it true, or only a rumour?', we have come to doubt each other so.

In Jersey the food situation is worse than Guernsey, only enough food for a few more days we hear and the troops are dying from gangrene, still the heads won't come to any agreement. A meeting has been held in Guernsey but the General there says, 'there is enough food in the Island to last until December', this includes us too. There has been no meat for three or four weeks. One is so tired and weary, even first thing in the morning. Norah is quite limp and hates going to school, she is always tired.

September 22nd, 1944

Today an English boat has been sailing round the Island flying a huge white flag, some say as big as a sheet. When near Guernsey, a small boat put out and took the German General on board for two hours. We are all quite thrilled and eagerly awaiting the results of this, we can talk of nothing else, I hope we are not disappointed again this time.

Our Harvest Festival was on Sunday and the church was packed with all sorts of sundries and vegetables galore. A padre came over from Guernsey for three days. The vegetables and oddments were sold by auction the next day. Mrs Hathaway sent a whole packet of candles and several dozen matches. I went to the sale hoping to buy a candle, but they were sold in twos and threes and each candle worked out about 3s or 4s each, and matches (one box) about the same. I could not possibly give that, I would rather do without a light at night and go to bed. A small tablet of Lux soap brought 52 marks (£5 12s 6d), think of it, ordinary prices in peace-time about 3d or 4d a tablet. The vegetables brought unheard-of prices and the Islanders bought them freely. You will say, no doubt, how do they have so much money? Well, men and women have been working for the Germans for four years and earning anything from £3 to £5 a week. So they can, and do, spend freely as fast as they earn it. Not so with us few English who are left behind, we have not got it to throw away and would rather go naked than work for the Germans.

The majority of them don't worry or want the war to cease, they have no loved ones on the other side to come back to, some have never been to England, it has no appeal to them. Just heard the sale (Harvest Festival) made £104, it is for ancient mariners and additional clergy fund, so someone will reap the benefit. Also just heard the boat carrying the white flag is supposed to come back in eight days, so the time is up tomorrow, how eagerly I shall watch the seas and wait results. In Jersey they are actually starving, also a break out of some sickness (not known), no medical things whatever and no anaesthetics.

In Guernsey it is said they can hold out another month. I wonder! Sark is supplied from there. The few bakehouses there cook what meals can be cooked and the people wait hours to get that done.

Some dismal Jimmies say we shall be here, and the Germans also, until the end of hostilities. Heaven forbid!

There is a gang of ruffians in Guernsey going about after dark and cutting off the girls' hair, shaving it nearly—the girls who have been carrying on with the Germans. There are hundreds of German babies there, the girls have gone crazy with the German soldiers.

October 4th, 1944

Another month started of our prison life and another month nearer to Christmas. This time last year I began cheering the folk up and telling them we would all be eating plum pudding for Christmas, it was quite a joke, and when I met friends they said, 'Now Mrs T. what about the Christmas pudding?', so this year I have grown wiser and sadder, and don't intend to prophesy, I am living a day at a time, all my nice dreams came to nothing.

The Germans are now exchanging their horses with the Sark farmers for fat cows, helping to feed them and prolonging the war. There is no doubt about it, this Island is not patriotic, they are selling all the while to the Germans and getting huge prices. I only hope afterwards the filthy marks they are banking will be worthless and so punish them. Sixty more Marines are coming to Little Sark today because they are still mining and fortifying.

Florrie Carré's little girl Nanette was killed yesterday, only four years old. She strayed on to a minefield just in sight of her own house. Two cousins near her were badly wounded with shrapnel. I wonder there have not been dozens of deaths before now, for we expected coasts to be mined but not up to our back and front doors. It is this awful feeling of being shut in, and shut off, that gets us most, we are all suffering from mental strain. Last night I dreamt I was at Kingston market, and in the market-place I can remember there being a shop that used to fascinate me, where the sausages were being cooked on a kind of grill in the shop window. I was just on the point of going in when I awoke.

If we could only know what was being done daily on all the fronts, things would be easier to bear, it is this uncanny silence or listening to lying rumours, that depresses us.

I had a letter from Mrs Russel today and she writes to say Mrs Greener (Colonel Greener's widow) is very ill. The rations in Guernsey for each person are $\frac{3}{4}$ pint skimmed milk and 1oz of butter, meat only every five or six weeks. In Jersey the poor souls are putting placards up in the streets saying, 'We are starving, you eat all our food, we had plenty before you came, clear out you swine.' As fast as notices are put up they are pulled down by the Germans, only to be rewritten and put up again.

In Guernsey the German General has put notices up saying, 'The civilians must not sell to the troops', but alas the Islanders are reaping a rich harvest out of the Germans and are in no hurry for the war to end. Because they keep selling to them the Germans are not being starved out, as they should be and England expects them to be, but they are living in luxury, comparatively speaking, so it amounts to this, that the Islanders are feeding the enemy and it is the few loyal ones who are suffering most.

Great excitement, I have found a little pot with ends of soap in (like those we used to keep to put in the copper on washing days), what a relief to have a proper wash. I certainly feel cleaner.

There has been heavy firing over Alderney for the last three days. A notice this week says, 'Anyone who has a fat cow to exchange for a horse, kindly communicate with the Commandant.' Twenty-three of the Germans' horses were killed last week to feed the troops.

October 6th, 1944

A plane this week has brought the troops letters from Germany, the airport at Guernsey has been tidied up. We also hear a Red Cross ship may come in the future but we have heard that tale for two years.

I have seen Mr Churchill's speech of September 28th, don't ask me how, it was lent to me, and I dare not say by whom. It was lovely to hear a bit of first-hand news and know it was really genuine, it was rather sad to hear we may go into 1945 but we are glad to know something definite. As the cold dark days draw near we shudder with the cold, all our clothes are worn threadbare especially undies, and shoes and stockings as well, the least said about them the better.

October 23rd, 1944

I do believe they definitely mean to starve us. Hitler says, 'no surrender, fight until the last', and the amazing thing is, there is no noise of strife going on here.

The following information has been published, probably to keep us quiet. 'The Channel Isles had virtually been cut off from all supplies already, a month before the invasion. From that moment the Islands lived on the produce of the Islands and from stocks which had been formed according to instructions from the occupying power. In view of the possibility of a state of siege, agriculture and industry has been adapted as far as feasible to make the fortresses self-supporting.

As the population, however, cannot be supplied indefinitely from the stocks of the fortresses or from the produce harvested or manufactured within them, the Commander of the Channel Islands some time ago took the precaution of getting in touch with a superior authority and has informed the German Government of the situation.

The action was appreciably facilitated by reports about the most essential commodities, supplies of which were running out in the near future, submitted by the States of Guernsey in the interest of the population of Guernsey.

The German Government has intimated its intention of taking the necessary steps in this matter with the protecting power. For this purpose the Commander of the Channel Isles has submitted a report about the Islands' monthly requirements of essential commodities.

Any action the protecting power may decide to take on this information is now, of course, beyond the control of the occupying authorities.'

Who the protecting powers are, goodness only knows, so we are even more confused.

October 28th, 1944

The Germans are killing more horses off and the cows the civilians have sold or exchanged will last them weeks, probably months.

They have also taken forty tons of beans off the States of Guernsey, food that was being kept for the people in the winter, also

I hear they have stolen sixty sheep. The Germans are boasting that they can hang out until next July. Heaven forbid!

It is pitiful the tales we hear from Guernsey. Most of the people have to stay in bed all day, there is no heat or light of any kind either to warm or cook by, no hot water can be had for toilet purposes or washing dishes, all has to be done in cold.

Someone has a notice up in Lanyon's window offering £50 for a few pounds of tobacco leaves. We hear the Bailiff's son in Jersey has got away to France with fifteen others, and I do hope by now he is in England telling them all of our situation. The Germans have taken the Bailiff (his father) and put him into prison.

October 31st, 1944

It is my birthday, and my wish and longing has not come true. Norah wrote me a birthday note saying, 'Many happy returns of the last birthday in captivity.' I wonder! I have caught a nasty cold and I cough incessantly but anyway, we spend most of the time in bed thank goodness, it is the only way to keep warm.

It is a strange situation revealing itself for, although the Germans are cornered here and are English prisoners, we are still German prisoners, and well we know it. Hitler says in his news-reel this week, 'Germany's enemy must be brought to realize that every yard they advance into our land will cause their blood to flow in torrents. Every block of houses, every village, every farm, every ditch, every bush, and every wood will be defended by the men and lads, and if need by, by the girls and women.' Alderney had a terrible bombardment yesterday and all night. B. Hurley (who has just returned from there) says they have a big hospital underground, ten or twelve feet of cement deep, store-rooms and all sorts of cubby-holes. We hear our hospitals in Guernsey and Jersey are reduced to paper bandages, and Ionette, who has crushed ribs (cart went over him), cannot be bandaged at all. His wife told me she had to take one of the curtains down to wrap round him as he was in so much pain. The Guernsey doctor says, 'Thousands of people will die before Christmas if no help comes.' We have just heard Captain Noyan has got away to England from Jersey.

November 3rd, 1944

Norah and I have had a narrow escape from being burnt alive. A huge oak beam in the dining-room chimney caught fire, it must have been smouldering for days. A big fire started in the attic, burning or smouldering all night. It took seven or eight of Stock's workmen and a chain of buckets of water two hours working incessantly to put it out. It is a blessing the rain-water tanks were full up for we could never have managed with the well-water which is low and very hard and slow to get up. I was alone, Norah had just gone to school, when I saw what looked like a black fog outside, then I heard the slates cracking on the house. How I got to Stock's and found the man, I don't know, but I said goodbye to my house on the way. You know there is no fire-escape, no hose, or anything to put fires out in Sark. We are living in one room on the west side of the house because all the other rooms are dripping with water. Strange to say, on my birthday night I said to Norah, 'Well, I have not exactly had a happy day, but it has been peaceful.'

We know we cannot now be marched off to Germany and that is the worst thing we feared, so we have much to be thankful for.

Little did we know then that this cursed thing would bring us a fire. You see about 8am when I started to light the fire it did go up in blazes. Then that cleared off and all seemed well until about 2pm when it broke out good and proper in the attic, the oak beam in the chimney burnt in the middle and the flaming ends fell down onto the attic floor. There is £30 or £60 lost but my insurance people left for England at the Occupation and I have not been able to pay the premiums so I don't know how we stand.

It was pathetic to see some of my birthday presents this year, a few onions, two or three tomatoes and a bit of salt.

November 13th, 1944

Night-time stealing still goes on and no one knows who is the thief. We have a few bad Sark boys who, I believe, help the Germans or put them wise as to where things are. I am lucky to have kept my pullets for so long as they do provide a little egg now and again.

We said this morning it is the thirteenth today and I hope it won't bring us bad luck and, lo, it has been a very lucky day. First thing in the morning a lady brought me a string of onions (they are like gold, we have onion gruel nearly every night), then when we were just sitting down to potatoes boiled in their jackets, another lady came in with a dish of stewed rabbit boiling hot which was very welcome, for the cold is intense and we could well have done without it just now (the cold I mean, not the rabbit). Then in the evening someone brought me an old saucepan for mine has been stolen from

face of real starvation. You may find it hard to believe but the troops are actually picking up cats and dogs they find in farmhouses and yards, and eating them. Two or three have fallen over the cliffs this week, some say they were limpeting to get some extra food, and others say they jumped over, the bodies have been taken to Guernsey for burial. They now have a piece of ground in Guernsey for burying, they have lost such a lot of men in the years they have occupied the Islands. In the early days a parson was asked in Guernsey if he would allow a German to be buried in his church-yard and he replied, 'Yes, as many as you like.'

The Admiral (from Guernsey) and several officers came over on Sunday and there was a kit inspection. How stupid, the men are in a rugged state with no smartness or attempt at it, they have no soap with which to shave or wash. We also hear that the Germans have taken over miles of glasshouses in Guernsey to plant early vegetables, so it would seem that as we are to receive Red Cross parcels now, relatively regularly, they mean to nip a bit more off the civilians.

Someone sent me a copy of the *Times Weekly* of April 1922. Oh, to see a real good English newspaper again!

We are told some of us old and weedy people here can be evacuated to Lisbon, but me thinks I will stay here until the end now, if it had been England I would pack at once.

January 30th, 1945

We hear, if it is true, that we are eighty miles from Berlin, the Russians anyway, so the time will not be long before we are in touch with the mainland again. The weather is very severe, the coldest I have known it in Sark and the wind is very strong. There is a lot of sickness with only half the children at school, chicken-pox, measles, scabies and others, no doctors to tend them and no drugs.

February 14th, 1945

Six weeks ago we had our first Red Cross parcels. We were told they would come every month but the boat was delayed, however, it arrived last week in Guernsey so we were hoping to have a lovely Valentine of lots of good food, but alas, our little Sark boat has not arrived. Never have I felt the hunger as I have this last fortnight. Saturday, when we got up, there wasn't a bit of bread or anything in the cupboard, these are grim, lean and hungry times for us all and still these Germans stick like leeches sucking our very existence.

They have started to plant corn and lots of potatoes, these will not be ripe until the autumn, do they really think we, or they, can carry on till then? It is a ghastly thought.

The Bailiff of Guernsey has written to Geneva, and the German Commandant has sent it, to say the situation is desperate. Since the Channel ports were closed in June last no food has come from France so the Islands are quite exhausted. The Germans were ordered by the Red Cross to supply the Islands until another Red Cross ship can arrive about the 4th or 5th of March, but the Germans won't, or either can't, supply them.

February 15th, 1945

Cheers, and once more, God bless the Red Cross!

I instantly put the kettle on and made a real cup of tea and managed to drink five cupfuls. I felt like the lady in Dickens, visibly swelling before his very eyes. If I ever manage to collect some money together I will make a handsome subscription to that splendid organization, the Red Cross. The lanes and shops were crowded with people again, carts and wheelbarrows were transformed with joy and gratitude waiting for the parcels to be given out.

February 24th, 1945

I have been reading back entries in my Diary and I see I hoped we should be relieved in 1940, what a hope! The waiting for freedom is long and tedious, although we know in our hearts the end is not so far off now but I have given up hoping, the days are getting more dreary. I suppose, as they say, 'Hope springs eternal in the human breast.' You are but eighty miles away, so near and yet so far. Even the call of spring with the daffodils and primroses showing don't gladden my heart as they always used to do, the waiting for so long, the tedium. There is no pomp and vanity about the troops now, no singing to order on the march, no marching at all, no parades, no shooting practice or any signs of soldiering. They are allowed to stay in bed until 10 or 11am to save a meal. They get a meal of soup and a slice of bread at 12 noon and no more until noon the next day, all so different from the first two or three years of the Occupation. The children are no longer compelled to learn German in the schools. Now the soldiers speak freely of being taken prisoner and I am sure the majority of them will welcome that.

March 1st, 1945

We have heard news of you from Ivor Pittard who is still in prison camp in Germany saying you are all well. Also a Red Cross message from Auntie Betty sent in June, 1944. The sun is shining once again.

These devils still hang on, in a starving state, and in Guernsey the troops are dropping down dead in the streets with starvation. We hear the ship will shortly arrive from Lisbon. It is no wonder we feel sick and giddy with malnutrition.

I feel in my bones we shall only be free when this war ends, or until the last of the troops fall down dead. Norah is getting very nervy and tired and I try to buck her up by saying, 'We may have peace for Easter.' The Union Jack and our red, white and blue favours are quite handy for the great day.

The daffodils, violets, freesia, stocks and wallflowers and primroses surpass themselves this year, I feel certain it is an omen of peace, and a speedy one, the sunshine is as warm as June, thank God for it. The planting of corn, roots and potatoes goes on in the fields and gardens although there is a great shortage of seeds, everyone relying on what was saved from last year's crop.

Our clocks were put on one hour on Sunday.

March 8th, 1945

We hear the *Vega*, the Red Cross ship, has arrived. I hope we receive the food before the Germans pinch it, for stealing goes on at a great rate. The troops are desperate, they come after dark tapping at the windows for any scraps of food, but it is fatal to begin to give it to one because one comrade tells another, but it is quite pitiful to see them, they have hardly strength to walk. This week Mrs Hathaway killed a pig for the Island's rations of meat but the Germans broke into the barn and cut pounds of it off with their bayonets.

March 17th, 1945

There has been a big fight in the Channel between Jersey and Granville, several boats put off from Jersey for Granville in search of food, reports say, and they captured some supplies and took back a lot of American prisoners. I wonder!!!

We hear the Channel Islands were spoken of on the BBC on

Sunday night and a service was held in Westminster Chapel, so we feel we are not forgotten. But oh, how long the time does seem of this prison life. They really ought to close the school because the children are well below par.

As soon as the Germans heard we were to have flour sent to Sark from Birkenhead (the place of my birth), they sent a ship over and took every scrap of corn and wheat back to Guernsey to have it ground for themselves. An order has gone round the Islands that civilians must only have ½ pint of milk each, they will take the rest.

The weather is getting warmer every day and the sun more powerful, all we want now is peace and the end of the war.

The Admiral in charge of troops in Guernsey is very much disliked by his officers and men—several attempts have been made on his life and although the men are starving he says he won't give in, they shall eat grass first he says. They have also had orders from Headquarters to keep the Channel Islands at all costs.

March 24th, 1945

This has been the most perfect March, hours and hours of sunshine with no gales. The primroses, daffodils and lilies are wonderful. Another attempt has been made on the Admiral's life in Guernsey because he will not erect the white flag. He came over here to inspect the troops and I noticed they were gunless, not surprising in that case. There is a little Pole here to whom I give lots of little titbits as I feel so sorry for him, he says he can't wait to get out of German uniform, they have been made to fight against their will.

March 30th, 1945

This is Good Friday, and everyone seems to be out gathering primroses and daffodils for the church decoration tomorrow. It is a wonderful sunny day and it gladdens one's heart, it would have been nice if peace could have come for this festive time, but we are told by someone who has a crystal set that it may come the end of April. I keep telling Norah she may get a real birthday letter for her birthday, who knows? She is enjoying her two weeks' holiday, taking gardening up for a change.

I have had a dose of flu for two weeks and feel wretched, and so depressed, it is all over the Island.

Sunday, April 1st, 1945

This is blessed Easter day, it must be over the fifth since Occupation. The little church looks wonderful, and although Easter was so early this year the primroses and daffodils have never been so plentiful or so lovely. Lots of willing workers helped to decorate it and a good many of the German troops kept coming in to see it and stood at the back of the church quite reverently, watching the work go on. No clergy can come over from Guernsey for two weeks and even then he must stay two weeks here, and it is not always convenient to him because a boat only comes to Sark once in two weeks on account of petrol shortage.

It is a real Robinson Crusoe Island and we feel it acutely, no news, no papers, only German lies. We hear that Berlin is soon to be entered by British troops. The Admiral came over again last week and told the troops they were lucky to be in Sark if even short of food, because, if they were in Germany they would be fighting on empty stomachs and that they must hold the fort here and never give up. One under-officer was heard to say, 'there would soon be no Germany to fight for', so he was carted off to prison camp in Guernsey. Cats and dogs still disappear. As the days and months go by we get more strung up than ever, the absence of news, true news, not lying rumours of Germany's victories, depresses us even more. A good many of these troops are not Nazis.

I am hoping for a speedy victory for all of us for everyone must be war-weary. The prisoners and those shut up like we are, not able to do a stroke towards victory, are to be pitied, we feel so helpless and can only stand and wait. We hope our Vicar has been sent to England and is now trying to forget his awful experiences. Miss Carter too will be amongst her friends at last.

April 7th, 1945

We hear the war is practically over and that Blackpool and Brighton were gay with holiday-makers at Bank Holiday. Cheers, but the German news would still have us believe that they are winning and they say, 'if Berlin is taken they will fight for these Islands.' So are we ever going to be free? They are rich in one thing, ammunition, we realize *that* when our planes fly over, the noise is terrific.

They have set up a dairy of their own, taken people's separators from them and are making cheeses, curds and butter by the pound, also they have taken our meat ration away. All this has happened since we received our last Red Cross parcels.

April 11th, 1945

I have bought a little batch of chickens, eleven, and I cannot tell you what joy it has given me, goodness knows what I am going to feed them on, but for two or three weeks they will eat so little. In the meantime I give them part of my bread ration each day, and who knows what may happen any day now, and a boat will come from England. At present we feel as though we are a thousand miles away from you.

Our little Sark boat is expected today bringing our Red Cross parcels.

Looking back in my Diary I said I could not stand another five months, that was in 1942, and now in 1945, we are going on in the same slow way, there seems no end to it, and as it gets nearer towards the close our nerves are becoming more frayed. The last new order is that 250 tons of wood must be cut in Sark to send to Alderney. The two lovely chestnut trees just opposite this house are both earmarked to come down, there is no beauty left anywhere in Sark, it is nearly bare.

I have managed to change my men's shoes size 8 for a pair of green suede boots, rather conspicuous. I can be seen a mile off and look like Puss-in-Boots. I dreamt last night I had arrived in England, but was in such a heavy sleep that no one could wake me up. Please God, don't let that happen.

April 19th, 1945

We have just heard President Roosevelt is dead, and feel so grieved, it is hard when the end must be so near not to have seen the results of all his labours.

We are daily expecting a fight for the Islands and there is a conference going on with the few remaining heads and we await eagerly the result. The Admiral who is so hated in Guernsey is reported missing. The troops in Guernsey are now stealing the civilians' Red Cross parcels.

April 24th, 1945

If we could only have our wireless to hear the good news and the peace celebrations, how happy I should feel. I would very much like to be in London, I wonder if it is very much damaged and altered. We have also heard all our armies have linked up and Berlin is surrounded, if it is true the end cannot be far off.

April 26th, 1945

It is Norah's birthday and she feels very sad, we both really believed that this year we should have met up with you and I had no present to give her. We are poorer than ever, our meat ration last week was 3d an oz each. Still no sign of the German troops putting up the white flag.

Yesterday thirty Russians were sent over to Sark from Guernsey, what for, goodness only knows, they are all billeted at the Arsenal and I hope they behave themselves. There have been four or five brutal murders in Guernsey, old folks living mostly alone found with their throats cut and all their food taken. It is supposed to be the troops but as there are so many nationalities there they can never trace it to them. It is a disgrace to any army or country to permit their troops to starve as these are doing instead of giving in, it is distressing to see the poor fellows walking about. They only have nettle soup now every day, they go about in groups with sacks gathering nettles, I don't think there are any potatoes or bread, it is slow starvation.

Saturday, April 28th, 1945

Today we hear that Mussolini is shot and all his followers, also that Hitler has had a stroke and will be dead in forty-eight hours and that the German troops are asking for peace and willing to give up the fight. I wonder if it is all true.

Sunday, April 29th, 1945

It is bitterly cold and snowing, and coming after a heat-wave in April, it is very hard to get used to it.

We hear today that the war is rapidly drawing to a close and any hour may bring PEACE.

May 1st, 1945

Still bitterly cold and snowing and still we are waiting for the good news and the Union Jack is standing by. Today we hear that Goering has shot himself.

May 2nd, 1945

Today we hear that the German Army in Berlin is giving up by the thousand and that the war is practically over.

May 3rd, 1945

The Red Cross ship went into Guernsey Harbour today and we are told it is her last trip to the Channel Islands. Soon I hope we shall have a boat from England.

The troops here look much happier because they see the end of the war is in sight.

The Admiral came over from Guernsey on the 1st May to address the troops, he told them Hitler was dead and that they must carry on here until the order to stop from his own Government arrives. Since then we hear, if it is true, that peace terms have been signed.

After all the dark days and being forced to listen to the lying rumours, it would be just heavenly to be in England and hear the bells and take part in the rejoicings for peace, if we only had our wireless to switch on we could hear most of it.

May 4th, 1945

We appear to be the last of the occupied countries to be freed, but as it gets to the end the feeling of relief is so great, and it makes it much more bearable, it has been a long weary five years with all its ups and downs and hopes and fears. I wonder whose letter I shall open first from you all, it will be quite thrilling to see an English stamp on it.

May 5th, 1945

We are expecting the white flag to go up any time. Strange to say we are none of us very excited as we thought we would be. Even now I cannot take it in, for it seemed one time it would never end.

May 6th, 1945

Our planes over Sark and Guernsey today, and the guns at Little Sark fired on them, the cheek of it, at this stage of the proceedings. They probably came to see if the white flag was up.

May 7th, 1945

We are all strung up and terribly excited as the glad hour comes nearer, we are certainly the last to be relieved, but oh, the joy, just to think it can really be happening. For five years now we could never speak freely or give vent in any way, but today the clouds seem higher and bluer, the birds are nearly bursting their little throats and all the world seems glad and looking forward to tomorrow for the final news.

Tuesday, May 8th, 1945

A NEVER TO BE FORGOTTEN DAY. The schools have two days' holiday and there has been a loudspeaker fitted up in the hall so that . . . (*May 9th missing.*)

May 10th, 1945

Plenty of food now because what food they had in reserve has been released since hostilities ceased. Flags are flying everywhere and the church bells have been ringing all day. No more blackouts, no more curfew, it seems too marvellous to be true, my brain won't take it in.

May 11th, 1945

Our troops have not arrived yet and the Germans are still with us helping to clear some of the horrible mess they have made everywhere, but they do not interfere with us and they are very quiet.

Don't laugh, one old gentleman (you know him) was married at 8am yesterday, he is getting on for ninety. I told you we were all dazed or crazy.

May 12th, 1945

A great day for Guernsey today, peace proclamation. Mrs Hathaway has gone over to represent Sark, every fishing boat has taken dozens of the inhabitants for the day. All our marks were changed today, 2s 1½d for every mark.

May 13th, 1945

I go into church every day and hold a little service to myself and thank God for all his goodness to me. If I kept on writing this Diary for ever I could never make you understand how thankful we all are for at last being relieved and free.

Chronology of the Occupation of the Channel Islands

17 June 1940   The Channel Islands were demilitarized. The Islanders were told to stay calm and offer no resistance in the event of an attack.

A vote was taken on each Island to decide whether or not to evacuate. Half the population of Guernsey, one-fifth of the people of Jersey, two men on Alderney and all 500 inhabitants of Sark decided to remain.

28 June 1940   Twenty-eight people killed by bombs and machine-gun-fire when German aeroplanes flew over the harbour at St Peter Port in Guernsey. The incident was known thereafter as 'The Battle of the Tomatoes' because of the damage to the fruit which was being loaded for export at the time.

30 June 1940   German advance party landed on Guernsey. The voluntary surrender of the Island was signed that night.

2 July 1940   German troops occupied Jersey.

3 July 1940   German troops occupied Sark and Alderney.

December 1941   A Lancaster bomber forced a landing near La Seigneurie.

During the first two years of the Occupation the number of German troops had increased, but now Hitler began to withdraw some of the best troops for service on the Russian Front. They were replaced by prisoners of war, mostly from Russia and Poland, who helped to build new fortifications.

September 1942   To reduce the number of mouths to be fed, the Germans issued an order that all those between the ages of sixteen and sixty who had not been born on the Islands would be deported. Eleven British residents living on Sark were sent to camps in Germany.

October 1942	Two Germans killed in British Commando raid on Sark.
	Also during 1942 radio sets were banned, but hidden receivers (cats' whiskers) kept the inhabitants informed of progress of the war elsewhere.
January 1943	Further deportees shipped to Germany, including the Dame of Sark's American husband.
November 1944	Bitterly cold. Starvation a real threat to the Islanders. In a desperate effort to beg for food and help two men attempted to escape to France in a fishing boat. They were picked up by an American destroyer.
December 1944	Answering the plea for help, a Red Cross ship, the SS *Vega*, called first at Guernsey then at Jersey to distribute 750 tons of food supplies.
6 May 1945	The Dame of Sark must have had her own sources of information because she hoisted the Union Jack and the American flag on the tower of La Seigneurie two days before the Bailiffs of Guernsey and Jersey were officially informed by the Germans that the war was over.
8 May 1945	Winston Churchill in his famous Victory Day speech mentioned the Islands, saying, 'Our dear Channel Islands are also to be freed today.'

Sources: Eggert, Harald *The Channel Islands* (Robert Hale); Hawkes, Ken *Sark* (David & Charles)

Biographical Note

The Island of Sark held a strong attraction for Julia Tremayne since she began taking her three young children there for regular school holidays, and so it was not surprising when, in her mid-forties, she decided to make the Island her permanent home. She and her family moved into a large house called Grand Dixcart, almost in the middle of the Island in the Dixcart Valley, which Mrs Tremayne soon set up as a guest house. It quickly gained a good reputation as her cooking was highly recommended and her polite, gentle yet firm manner made people respect her. Her warm hospitality was renowned.

Julia Tremayne was small with dark brown eyes and long black hair kept in a bun or tied in a plait, and she had tremendous energy, working incessantly to look after the house and her young family. She used to wear long dresses or suits, always in dark colours, but she would dress them up with a necklace or brooch and usually a pair of earrings. The garden was her delight and she looked after it with great care and attention. She grew many vegetables which were an invaluable source of food during the German Occupation as were her hens' eggs, although their supply was unreliable. She also kept some goats for their milk so that when she was not working in the house she would be outside tending her animals and garden.

Mrs Tremayne stayed at Grand Dixcart until after the War when she moved to Petit Dixcart, also in the Dixcart Valley. Her letters to her daughter Betty who was in England, relate the hardships she and her elder daughter Norah, along with the rest of the Sarkees, had to endure while the Germans were occupying Sark, but they also describe the tremendously strong bond of friendship that existed between the Islanders during those tormenting five years. They all tried desperately hard under the most difficult conditions to support each other and to remain cheerful even during the most harrowing moments, and they would offer their last spoonful of tea to anyone whose need was greater than their own.

Even when confronted by her own daughter's desperate pleas to destroy the letters, Mrs Tremayne was determined that they should eventually reach their destination, and she therefore bravely undertook to hide them in Grand Dixcart not only from the Germans, who would have severely punished her had they found them, but also from her daughter. As Norah and her mother were seldom apart during the years of the Occupation, it was not easy for Mrs Tremayne to find an excuse and the time almost every day to escape on her own to record the day's events.

The Germans took a number of the Sarkees off the Island during the Occupation and sent them to prison camps, where food, clothing and blankets were more plentiful than on the Island. The people left behind on Sark felt inevitably that it would be their turn next to be transported, and Julia Tremayne believed this more than anybody since she was of British nationality. This final humiliation, though, was denied her and was due, she thought, to the fact that Norah taught in the school and spoke fluent German and French which she used to advantage by acting as interpreter. Although the Tremaynes were badly impoverished during the War, they helped the less fortunate Islanders, and Mrs Tremayne's generous nature would not allow her to turn away some starving Germans who came begging at her door for any small scraps of food she was able to spare them.

As a result of war and the ensuing occupation, Mrs Tremayne was completely cut off from regular news of the rest of her family which was a burden she found increasingly difficult to bear. Her two grandchildren were born during the War and, when she started knitting some clothes for her first baby granddaughter, she was heart-broken when a friend told her she would do better to make something for a fourteen-year-old. Red Cross messages were few and took a long time to filter through so Norah and her mother were never up to date with any news from England and, after their wirelesses were taken away, they could never rely on anything written in the newspapers as these were full of German propaganda.

At the end of the War Julia Tremayne did not abandon the Island she now considered her home but stayed there for about another ten years. She then returned to England and stayed with her daughter Betty in the West Country where she died in her late eighties. Her letters remain as a fitting tribute to this warm-hearted, humorous and generous lady, and a remarkable eye-witness account of life under the Occupation.

Acknowledgements

The publishers would like to thank the following for supplying illustrations:

Michael Beaumont, Seigneur of Sark: 66, 67 (above); Mrs Jane Cox: 73 (below left), 135 (below), 142; Xan Franks: 65 (above); Guernsey Museum (W. F. Tipping): 77, 130, 131 (above), 139, 144; Imperial War Museum: 134 (above); Carel Toms: all other photographs.